BREAK 'N

WINDOWS

The Adventures of Blinky and Ibby

| I ⊙ ☑ ▾ ↔ ↕ ↖ ⊘ I |

BREAK'N

WINDOWS

A WINDOWS-WORD REALLY-QUICK
USER-FRIENDLY REFERENCE MANUAL
FOR BEGINNERS & OTHERS

The Adventures of Blinky and Ibby

by Bob Ginsberg

| I ⊙ ☑ ▾ ↔ ↕ ↖ ⊘ I |

About the Book
(condensed from the Foreword)

The Title:
   Before a military headquarters sends a message to one of its units it encrypts the message so that only friendly forces with the key to the code can decipher it. When someone else finds out how the code works he or she is said to have broken the code. For many beginners the computer instruction books seem to be in code. The title of this book, **BREAK'N WINDOWS,** tells the novice that the code has been broken and that this reference manual can be readily understood.

The reason this manual was written:
   This manual was initially developed for the purpose of giving the author quick and easy directions for common computer operations. He wanted a book from which he could get the information quickly and easily. When friends learned about his simpler way they insisted that he share his manual with them.

The scope of this manual:
   This book is not definitive; it treats common operations and only those that can be presented in a reasonably short space. A few very useful topics with much longer explanations are given in the appendices; the rest of them are listed with the advice: "See a bigger book".

Table of Contents

Foreword

The Title:
   Before a military headquarters sends a message it encrypts the message so that only friendly forces with the key to the code can decipher it. When someone else finds out how the code works he or she has "broken the code". For many people, computer instruction books seem to be in code. The title of this book, **BREAK'N WINDOWS,** tells the novice that the code has been broken and that this reference manual can be readily understood.

The reason this manual was written:
   This manual was initially developed for the purpose of giving the author quick and easy directions for common computer operations. Unlike some children he does not remember each simple routine as he first learns it. He owns a number of thick books, each of which has much of the information but none of which has all the information. Even if one of the books had all the information he is too impatient to wade through six pages of text to locate a few simple directions. When friends learned of his simpler way to get computer directions they insisted that he share his manual with them.

The scope of this manual:
This work is not meant to be definitive;
it treats common operations and only
those that can be presented in a
reasonably short space. A few very
useful operations with longer explanations are given in the appendices; the
rest of them are listed with the advice:
See a bigger book.

Use of non-standard terms:
A few computer terms in common use were
considered misleading or ambiguous and
were replaced for clarity. Consider the
word "select". For more than a thousand
years the verb has meant "to choose".
Computer people use it to mean "Choose
some text and highlight it". The author
confesses that after knowing such usage
for more than a month he still failed to
respond properly to the word "select"; a
habit of some 66 years is hard to break.
The problem is further compounded
because computer people also use the
word "select" in the usual way when
they mean only "to choose".
   To replace "select" the author uses
"hilite", a term that describes the act
with clarity and with the imagery of a
person using a hilite pen.

What is a memory?

The author once heard someone say: "... and put it into memory." The author asked "Which memory?" He was told "There is only one memory!" Now the word memory implies a device to store information and the author had several such devices in his computer: Floppy Disk, CD ROM, Hard Drive, Zip Drive, and Jaz drive. The person was, of course, referring to none of these; he was referring to the RAM or random access memory which is a rapidly accessible memory but hardly a long term storage device. This is another bit of computer terminology that causes difficulty for the beginner.

Blinky and Ibby The standard names "Insertion Point Cursor" and "I-Beam Mouse Pointer" are descriptive but unwieldy when used so frequently. They have been replaced by "Blinky", a term whose imagery is apparent, and "Ibby", a term which is to be preferred here over the abbreviation "IBM". The use of "Blinky" and "Ibby" and a few other departures from standard usage is in no way meant to minimize the great achievements of Windows and of the Microsoft company. They are only used to make this manual more user friendly.

Lines the readers can use to add their own information:

Some of the author's friends admitted that they too make notes for remembering seldom-used computer routines. Where blank spaces would have occurred on the pages of this manual marked by the alphabet, lines have been provided so that each person can add his or her own personal instructions.

Hopefully this manual will be of use.

It is hoped that the use of this manual will help the beginner to use the computer more efficiently and with less frustration, and that it will enable the more advanced user to get some quick directions to answer an occasional question.

CAUTION   *CAUTION*

1.0 DO NOT TURN OFF YOUR COMPUTER UNTIL YOU
Click Start, Click Shut Down. When asked "Are you sure you want to ⊙ shut down the computer?" Click Yes and WAIT until you are told that it is safe to shut down.

2.0 Never delete anything you haven't created.

3.0 Install an efficient surge suppressor between your computer power plug and the wall socket.

4.0 Prepare an Emergency Start-up Disk.
(See "emergency start-up disk" under **E**.)

5.0 When you make a mistake PR Ctrl+Z to undo it.

CAUTION   *CAUTION*

Notes

Buttons, Rulers and Drop-Down Menus

<u>Figures 1 and 2</u> show and tell about almost all of the items on the MsWord window. Most of the commands in this manual refer to these items.

<u>Figure 3</u> lists the contents of all the menus that drop down when you click the titles on the menu bar.

Study the figures and become well acquainted with them. (Of course when you are using MsWord and you rest the arrow on an item its name will usually appear, and when you click a title on the menu bar the drop-down menu appears.)

This manual assumes:

1. that you have a mouse.
2. that the standard toolbar and the formatting toolbar are present when using MsWord. Other toolbars can be inserted as needed. See "toolbars" under **T**.
3. that the icons for much used folders and programs appear on the desktop, including MsWord. See "shortcut.. Create a shortcut." under **S**.
4. that you have set up a group of useful folders. See "folders..Set up a group of useful folders." under **F**.

Capitalization, Punctuation & Use of Non-Standard Words in This Manual

Abbreviated commands such as CL, PR, etc. will be capitalized. Others such as Copy, Drag, etc. will be capitalized only when they start a sentence. Titles of buttons and menus will be capitalized as they are on the buttons and menus. Items such as icon, toolbar, etc. will not be capitalized unless they begin a sentence or appear in a title.

New Words
In the rare case where a word in Windows usage is unclear or misleading a new word has been used. For example the ambiguous word "select" has been replaced with the clear and colorful word "hilite". Non-standard words are defined in the list of abbreviations and key words .

Quotes for Clarity
When an item be clicked upon has two or more words in its name they will appear in quotes for clarity.

_____

_____

_____

_____

_____

_____

_____

_____

Seemingly Redundant Instructions
At times you will have onscreen a group of dialog panels and the next instruction will be to CL the tab of one of the panels (to bring it up front). Sometimes that panel is already up front! In that case ignore the instruction; it appears in the manual for those cases where the desired panel may be hidden.

Problems?
See Appendix 1 for help with some common problems. If that fails see a bigger book, phone the company that sold you your software or that sold you your computer with your software. If you still have problems talk to a friend who is a computer expert.

_____

_____

_____

_____

_____

_____

_____

_____

_____

_____

_____

_____

_____

Abbreviations & Key Words

AOL   American Online, Inc., a network provider.

arrow   ⬉ The tilted white arrow is one form of mouse pointer. See "mouse pointers" under **M** for other forms.

Blinky | Blinky is a more descriptive term for "insertion point cursor", the blinking vertical line that tells you where your typing will appear.

CL   Click the left mouse button when the arrow tip or other pointer is on the item (button, tab, icon, frame, etc).

checkbox ☑ When a checkbox contains a check mark the instructions to its right will be implemented.

CLHold Click & hold down the left mouse button when the arrow tip or other pointer is on the item (button, tab, icon, frame, etc)..

CLClear   If a radio button ⊙ contains a dot or if a check box ☑ contains a check mark CL the button or box to remove the dot or check mark.

CL X   Click the Close button **X** on the right end of the Title bar to delete the window.

cursor The cursor is an onscreen symbol that moves when the mouse is moved. Blinky ▎and Ibby I are usually called cursors. The arrow, ↖ double-arrow ↕,↔, etc. are usually called pointers. Here Blinky and Ibby will be called Blinky and Ibby and the other cursors will be called pointers. See "mouse pointers" under **M**.

DBLCL Double-click the left mouse button when the arrow tip or other pointer is on the item (button, tab, icon, frame, etc).

double-arrow ↕ or ↔ or **tilted 45°**. These are used to drag an edge or a corner to change the size of a window.

down arrow ▼ This often appears at the right end of a frame on a dialog panel (box). Click it and a list appears.

Drag   Move an item or text using a pointer. See "Drag....." under **D**.

Embed Paste an item & its program.

Abbreviations

Esc key   The escape key works like CL Cancel.

frame   A frame is a rectangular opening on a dialog panel (box).

Hilite (highlight for the purist) is a more descriptive term for "Select". See "Hilite text" under **H**.

Ibby I Ibby is the I-Beam mouse pointer that shows where Blinky is hiding and with a click makes Blinky appear.
(Do not abbreviate as IBM.)

Link   Several programs share the same version of an object.

menu   A menu is a list of options from which you can choose.

Move the arrow.   Move the mouse to move the arrow. The mouse also moves the other pointers.

mouse   The mouse is a device the size of a bar of soap which when moved on a surface causes the pointer on the screen to move in the same direction.

 On some computers the mouse is replaced by a trackball, a trackpoint, or a touchpad which do the same thing. When used here the word mouse means the actual mouse or a substitute.

Ms®   Microsoft®, a registered Trademark.

panel   The word "panel" is a more descriptive term for "dialog box".

Place Blinky.   If the command is to "Place Blinky" somewhere, then move Blinky to that location by either
1. using the arrow keys or
2. moving Ibby to that location and clicking to produce Blinky.

pointer   See "cursor" above and "mouse pointers" under **M**.

PR   Press and release a keyboard key.

PR Alt+F (for example)   Press and hold down Alt and Press F.

PR ALT,F,A (for example) Press Alt, then Press F, then Press A.

PR Ctrl+A (for example)   Press and hold down Ctrl and Press A.

PRHold Press & hold down a keyboard key.

radio button ⊙ When a radio button contains a dot the instructions to its right will be implemented.

RAM Random Access Memory but what is more important it is Rapidly Accessible Memory.

RAO Rest Arrow On.

RTCL Click the right mouse button when the arrow tip or other pointer is on the item (button, tab, icon, frame, etc). A helpful menu usually appears.

RTDrag Move the arrow until its tip rests on the item to be dragged. Click & hold down the right mouse button. Move the item to its new location. Release the mouse button.

used paper Paper that has print on one side can be used for testing or for preliminary layouts, etc. Don't use paper that has a lot of ink on it from graphics, logos, etc. because it might be warped enough to jam the printer.

W'Explorer Windows Explorer

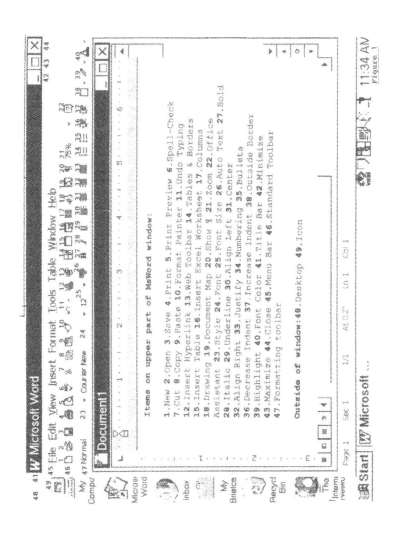

Figure 1. Items on Upper Part of MsWord Window

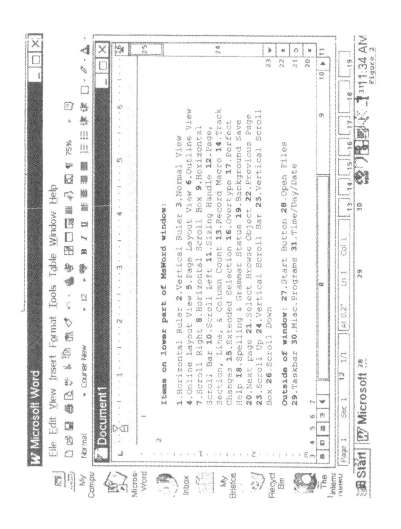

Items on lower part of MsWord window:

1.Horizontal Ruler 2.Vertical Ruler 3.Normal View
4.Online Layout View 5.Page Layout View 6.Outline view
7.Scroll Right 8.Horizontal Scroll Box 9.Horizontal
Scroll Bar 10.Scroll Left 11.Sizing Handle 12.Page,
Section, Line, & Column Count 13.Record Macro 14.Track
Changes 15.Extended Selection 16.Overtype 17.Perfect
Help 18.Spelling & Grammar Status 19.Background Save
20.Next page 21.Select Browse Object 22.Previous Page
23.Scroll Up 24.Vertical Scroll Bar 25.Vertical Scroll
Box 26.Scroll Down

Outside of window: 27.Start Button 28.Open Files
29.Taskbar 30.Misc.Programs 31.Time/Day/Date

Figure 2. Items on Lower Part of MsWord Window

File	Edit	View	Insert	Format	Tools	Table	Window	Help
New	Undo Typing	Normal	Break	Font	Spelling & Grammar	Draw Table	New Window	MSoft Word Help
Open	Repeat Typing	Online Layout	Page Numbers	Paragraph	Language	Insert Table	Arrange All	Contents & Index
Close	Cut	Page Layout	Date and Time	Bullets & Numbering	Word Count	Delete Cells	Split	What's This?
Save	Copy	Outline	AutoText	Borders & Shading	AutoSummarize	Merge Cells	1Document1	
Save As	Paste	Master Document	Field	Columns	AutoCorrect	Split Cells		MSoft on the Web
Versions	Paste Special	Toolbars	Symbol	Tabs	LookUp Reference	Select Row		WordPerfect Help
Page Setup	Paste as Hyperlink	Ruler	Comment	Drop Cap	Track Changes	Select Column		About MSoft Word
Print Preview	Clear	Document Map	Footnote	Text Direction	Merge Documents	Select Table		
Print	Select All	Header & Footer	Caption	Change Case	Protect Document	AutoFormat		
Send To	Find	Footnotes	Cross-reference	AutoFormat	Mail Merge	Distr. Rows Evenly		
Properties	Replace	Comments	Index & Tables	Style Gallery	Envelopes & Labels	Distr. Col. Evenly		
	Go To	Full Screen	Picture	Style	Letter Wizard	Cell Height & Width		
	Links...	Zoom	Text Box	Background	Macro	Headings		
	Object		File	Object	Templates & Add-Ins	Convert Text to Table		
1C:\WINDOWS\DESKTOP\Bob's\Blinky1			Object			Sort		
2C:\WINDOWS\DESKTOP\Bob's\Blinky2			Bookmark		Customize	Formula		
3C:\WINDOWS\DESKTOP\Bob's\Blinky3			Hyperlink		Options	Split Table		
4C:\WINDOWS\DESKTOP\Bob's\Blinky4						Show Gridlines		
Exit								

Drop down menus from the Microsoft Word Menu Bar

Figure 3

Figure 3. MsWord Menu Bar Drop-Down Menus

access numbers for AOL To change the access phone numbers CL the AOL icon, CL Setup, CL "Edit Location", type the new numbers in the "phone numbers" frames. Enter 1 for # of tries on each phone. (It's the number of tries before they try the other number!)

addresses The big books tell you how to make and use an address book but it often requires a program you don't have. If you wish you can create a simple but useful address file in Word: Type a large, bold letter **A** and underneath it list the names starting with A and their addresses, phone numbers, fax numbers and Email addresses. Repeat for the entire alphabet. Save the document with the name "Addresses". In the Normal View layout your address list will appear as on a continuous roll of paper.

addresses on envelopes To use your list to print names and addresses on envelopes see Appendix 9.

addresses on labels To print a name and address on a label scroll through your address list until you find the desired address. Hilite the address (but not the phone number, fax number or Email address). CL Copy, CL **X**. The address is now on your clipboard. See Appendix 2. On your label form place

Blinky where you want the address to appear and CL Paste.

Align text. (Align left, Center, Align right, or Justify).
To type with your choice of alignment: CL one of the four alignment buttons on the formatting tool bar and type. To type with a different choice CL a different button.
To change the alignment of an existing block of text: hilite the text and CL one of the four alignment buttons.

Arrange icons. RTCL the folder window, CL "Arrange Icons". For alphabetical arrangement, CL "by Name". Otherwise CL "by Type", or CL "by Size", or CL "by Date".

Arrange windows. RTCL Clock. CL Cascade, or CL "Tile Horizontally", or CL "Tile Vertically".

AutoCorrect. If you have problems with an automatic feature of the program you may be able to remove that feature. CL Tools, CL AutoCorrect, CL the AutoCorrect tab. CLClear to remove the checkmarks from any or all of the five automatic boxes. CL OK.

automatic indent See indents.

Automatically backup your files. CL Tools, CL Options, CL the Save tab.

CL the "Always Create Backup Copy" check-box, CL the "Save AutoRecovery info every" checkbox and CL the number of minutes between saves (10 for example). CL OK.

AutoText is a place to store often used text and graphics for quick access. Store something in AutoText: hilite it, CL Tools, CL AutoCorrect, CL the AutoText tab. Note that in the "Enter AutoText entries here" frame a name has been chosen for your entry; to change it place Blinky in the frame and edit or replace the name. CL Add. CL the right margin.
Retrieve something from AutoText: Place Blinky where you want the material, CL Tools, CL Auto-Correct, CL the AutoText tab, scroll to and CL the desired entry, CL Insert.
Delete an entry from Autotext: CL Tools, CL AutoCorrect, CL the AutoText tab. Scroll to and CL the entry you want to delete. CL Delete, CL OK, CL the right margin.

_____

_____

_____

_____

_____

_____

background for the desktop
See "wallpaper" under **W**.

background for online documents If you
want to spice up your online documents
with a colored, textured, or patterned
back-ground: CL Format; CL Background;
CL a color for a colored background, or
CL "More Colors" to create a custom
color, or CL "Fill Effects" for
Gradient, Texture, Pattern or Picture
backgrounds. (If you create too vivid a
background the recipient of your online
document may not be able to read the
message, especially if they do not have
a color printer.) For more information
see a bigger book.

Backup a file or folder. See "Copy a
file from one drive to another." and see
"Copy a folder from one drive to
another.".

Backup files automatically. CL Tools,
CL Options, CL the Save tab. CL the
"Always Create Backup Copy" checkbox,
CL the "Save AutoRecovery info every"
checkbox and CL in the number of minutes
between saves. CL OK.

**Begin a paragraph with a large capital
letter.** See "Start a paragraph with a
large fancy letter."

bitmap image (Paint Screen): RTCL the
Desktop, Cl New.

Blinky | Blinky is a blinking cursor that shows where the next character will be typed. Blinky can be moved up, down, left, and right by pressing the arrow keys; to move more quickly hold the arrow keys down. To move Blinky even more quickly to the end of the line PR End, to the beginning of the line PR Home. When Blinky is far from where you want him use the mouse to place Ibby there and then CL to produce Blinky. Then move Ibby a few lines up to avoid confusion.

bold, italic & underlined type To type with one or more of these effects CL the **B**, *I*, and/or U̲ buttons on the toolbar and type. To stop using them while typing CL the button/buttons again. To add one or more of these effects to existing text: hilite the text, CL the desired button or buttons, CL the right margin. To remove one or more of them from existing text: hilite the text, CL the proper button or buttons, CL the right margin.

> **Note:** Sometimes backspacing returns the previous setting! Sometimes entering a certain area of text returns the previous setting! Blame the automated programs.

B 3

Note: If the buttons are not on the toolbar CL Format, CL Font, CL the Font tab, CL your choices, CL OK. Notice how much easier it is when the icon is on the toolbar.

breaks, line & page   See "page breaks" under **P** and "line breaks" under **L**.

buttons   Buttons are square or rectangular areas on which you CL to give commands. Radio buttons ⊙ are small circles in the middle of which you CL to add a dot or CLClear to remove it. When the dot is there the instructions to the right will be implemented. The check box ☑ is similar but it is square and uses a check mark instead of a dot.

_____

_____

_____

_____

_____

_____

_____

_____

_____

_____

capital letters (upper case) Hilite the text. PRHold Shift. PR F3 repeatedly to go from all caps to no caps to first caps. When satisfied CL the right margin.

Change a word to another word throughout a document. CL Edit, CL Replace. In the "Find what" frame type the word you want to replace. PR Tab. In the "Replace with" frame type the desired word. CL "Replace all". When a note appears telling you that the replacements have been made CL OK.

Change from a display of large file icons to a more legible list of file names.
With the file icons showing in a folder window CL View, CL List.

Change the color or size or type font of buttons, title bars, window borders, etc.. See "display appearance items" under **D**.

Change the default settings for margins.
(Default means what you get if you don't do anything about it.)
If you don't like the margins that the program has chosen you can, of course, change them at any time. However if you would like to change them so they appear automatically then do the following:
DBLCL MsWord. CL File, CL "Page Setup",

CL the "Paper Size" tab. In the "Paper Size" frame CL ▼, scroll to and CL your paper size. CL Portrait for letters or CL Landscape for spreadsheets, etc.. In the "Apply to" frame if it doesn't say "Whole document" CL ▼, CL "Whole Document".

CL the Margins tab. CL to set the desired margins (if you can't decide a reasonable compromise is 1" for top, bottom, left, and right with 0" for headers and footers. In the "Apply to" frame if it doesn't say "Whole document" CL ▼, CL "Whole Document". In the lower left corner of the panel CL Default. When the sign asks "Do you want to change the default settings for page setup?" CL Yes. CL **X**. Your desired margins should now appear when you start a new document. If not, see Appendix 8.

Change the default settings for type font.

If you don't like the type font and type size that the program has chosen you can, of course, change them at any time. However if you would like to change them so they appear automatically then do the following:

DBLCL MsWord. CL Format, CL Font, CL the Font tab. In the Font frame scroll to and CL the desired font. In the "Font Style" frame CL either Regular, or

Italic or Bold Italic. In the Size Frame
Cl the desired size. In the lower left
of the Font panel CL Default. When the
sign says,for example, "Do you want to
change the default font to Courier New,
12 pt?" and that is the desired font
CL Yes. CL **X**. Your desired type font
should now appear when you start a new
document. If not, See Appendix 8.

**Change the mouse properties and
appearance.**
See "mouse properties" under **M**.

**Change the name of a file (and its
icon).** CL MyComputer, DBLCl the drive
the file may be on, DBLCL the folders
until the file's icon appears. CL the
icon, CL File, CL Rename. Type a new
name. PR Enter. Note: If the full name
isn't accepted, put an empty space at
the end of the first line and try again.

Change the size of a window. Point the
arrow at the lower right corner of the
window until the arrow becomes a tilted
double arrow. Drag the corner to change
the size. To change the <u>width</u> of a
window point the arrow at the right edge
of the window until the arrow becomes a
horizontal double arrow and drag the
edge. To change the <u>height</u> of a window
point the arrow at the bottom edge of
the window until the arrow becomes a
vertical double arrow and drag the edge.

Change the size or color or type font of buttons, title bars, window borders, etc. See "display appearance items" under **D**.

Change the type font, type size, etc. See "type font.. Replace." under **T**.

characters See "symbols and characters" under **S**.

Choose a type font. See "type font.. Choose." under **T**.

Clip Art See Appendix 6.

clipboard To view its contents DBLCL MsWord, CL Paste. Then to save it see "Store a document" under **S**.

Close a window. CL **X**.

color of icon title backgrounds, color of title bars, etc. See "display appearance items" and "wallpaper".

columns To set up a document in columns CL Format, CL Columns. In the Presets area CL the figure for two or three equal width columns or two unequal width columns with the narrower column on the left or right. For four or more columns: In the "Number of columns" area CL the arrows for the desired number. For equal width columns CL to put a check mark in the "Equal column width" checkbox. Otherwise CL the arrows to choose the width and spacing of each column separately. To put a vertical line between the columns CL to put a checkmark in the "Line between" checkbox. When satisfied CL OK.

control panel To view its contents DBLCL "My Computer", DBLCL "Control Panel".

Copy a clipboard onto a document. Place Blinky where you want the material to be inserted. CL Paste.

Copy a disk on a disk of the same type, such as Floppy to Floppy. Insert the "full" disk. DBLCL My Computer. RTCL the icon of the disk drive. CL CopyDisk. In the "Copy to" frame CL the same type of disc. CL Start. When told, install the blank disk. CL OK.

Copy a disk on a different type of disk, such as Floppy to Zip.
Insert the "full" disk. DBLCL My Computer, DBLCL the "full" disk drive. In the drive window CL Edit, CL "Select All", RTCL one of the icons. CL Copy. (The material goes to RAM.) On the "My Computer" screen DBLCL the drive where you want the material to be located. CL the folder where you want the material to be located; it will turn blue. RTCL it, CL Paste.

Copy a file from one drive to another using Save As panel. With the file on screen CL File, CL Save As. In the "Save in" frame CL ▼. In the large frame DBLCL the drive to receive the file, DBLCL the desired folder in that drive, DBLCL the sub-folder, etc. until the folder to receive the file appears in the "Save in" box. CL Save.

Copy a file from one window to another. With both windows showing, PRHold Ctrl, CLHold the icon of the file to be copied and drag it to the other window. Release.

Copy a file to the clipboard. Hilite the entire file (CL Edit, CL "Select All".) CL Copy. **or** RTCL the file's icon, CL Copy.

Copy a folder (call it folder g) from one drive to another using W'Explorer. CL Start, RAO Programs, CL W'Explorer. On the left side of the window CL the drive that holds folder g (or the folder on that drive that contains folder g) until folder g appears on the right side. On the left side bring into view the drive (or the folder on that drive) that will receive folder g. Drag folder g from the right side to its receiving drive or folder on the left.

Copy a window to the clipboard.
PR Alt+PrintScreen

Copy text at a nearby place. Hilite the
text, PRHold Ctrl and drag the hilite to
the second location. Also see:"Insert a
file in a document."

Copy text to the clipboard.
Hilite the text, CL Copy.

Copy text at a faraway place. Hilite
the text, CL Copy. Place Blinky in the
faraway place where you want the copy.
CL Paste. Note that once something is on
the clipboard it can be pasted again and
again until something else is cut or
copied to the clipboard.

Copy text from document 1 into document 2.
On document 1 hilite the text to be
copied, CL Copy, CL **X**. Bring document 2
to the screen. Place Blinky. CL Paste.
Also see "Insert a file into a
document." under **I**.

Copy the screen to the clipboard.
PR PrintScreen.

Create a page full of horizontal lines.
PRHold the shift key and PRHold the
under-line key to create a few lines.
Hilite the lines and CL Copy. CL the
right margin. CL Paste repeatedly until
the page is full of lines.

Use this method any time you want to repeat something quickly.

Create a folder.   See "folder.. Create." under **F**.

cursor, insertion point
                        See Blinky under **B**.

Cut text to the clipboard.   Hilite the text, CL Cut. Note that once something is on the clipboard it can be pasted again and again until something else is cut or copied to the clipboard.

Customize buttons, title bars, window borders, etc..   See "display appearance items.. Change." under **D**.

Customize the mouse's properties and the appearance of its pointers. See "mouse properties" under **M**.

_____

_____

_____

_____

_____

_____

_____

_____

day and date.. View. To view the day and date DBLCL the taskbar clock.

day, date, and time.. Set. To set the day, date, and time: DBLCL the taskbar clock, CL the correct date on the calendar, CL ▼ on the month box, CL the correct month, CL the up or down arrow to correct the year. PR Tab until the hour in the time box is hilited, erase the old hour and type in the correct hour. PR Tab, set the minutes one minute fast, PR Tab, set the seconds to zero, PR Tab, set AM or PM. When the time is exact CL OK.

daylight savings, auto adjust.. Set. RTCL the taskbar clock, CL "Adjust Date/Time." CL the "Time Zone" tab, CL ▼, CL the correct time zone, CL to put a checkmark in "Automatically adjusts for daylight savings changes". CL OK.

default option When confronted with strange choices PR Enter.

default settings The program has chosen a particular type font, type size, margin settings, etc. for your use when starting a new document. You may, of course, change any or all of these "default" settings at any time. However to have your personal choices appear automatically every time you start a new document you can follow the procedure given under "Change the default settings for margins." under **C,** and "Change the default settings for type font." under **C**. If that still doesn't work see Appendix 8 "Change the default type font and margins".

Delete a file or folder. CLHold the file icon & drag it to Recycle Bin.

Delete a lot of text at the start of a document. Place Ibby at the end of the text you want to delete. CLHold and drag up and to the left until the pointer reaches the upper boundary of the screen; the hilited text will then fly by very quickly. At the start of the document, release. CL Cut.

Delete a lot of text at the end of a document. Place Ibby at the start of the text you want to delete. CLHold and drag down and to the right until the pointer reaches the lower boundary of the screen; the hilited text will then fly by very quickly. At the end of the document, release. CL Cut.

_____

_____

_____

_____

Delete "Headers" (routing data) from the end of an e-mail letter before printing it.

Method 1. While online save the letter in your offline e-mail folder and edit it later when offline. See "Save an e-mail in an offline folder while online." under **S**.

Method 2. Using the clipboard, take the entire document offline to edit. While online place the arrow inside the letter and CL it. CL Edit, CL "Select All", CL Edit again, CL Copy, CL the **X** at the top right corner of the monitor. **Wait.** DBLCL MsWord, CL Paste. Hilite the unwanted "Headers", CL Cut, CL Print.

Deleted a file by mistake? DBLCL the Recycle bin. A list appears. Drag the title of the desired file to the desktop; its icon appears on the desktop. On the Recycle Bin list CL **X**. DBLCL the icon and the file appears in the MS Word window. See: "Save a file".

Delete recurring unwanted additions from e-mail, such as <BR>. Follow the directions in "Replace a word with another word" under **R** but leave the "Replace With" frame blank.

Delete hiliting. CL the right margin.

desktop background See "wallpaper".

dialog panels (boxes) Dialog panels let you choose options. When choices are preceded by small circles (radio buttons) or small squares (check boxes) you can choose an option by clicking the circle or square, thereby inserting a dot or check mark. Another click removes the dot or check mark (and the choice).

Some dialog panels have frames for typing in an entry. Some frames have move-up and move-down arrows. Click an arrow to move up or down a list to get the desired entry. Some frames have move-up and move-down arrows for increasing or decreasing a number: if the number you want isn't listed place Blinky by the number shown, erase it and type in your desired number.

Some frames have a down arrow ▼ ; CL it to produce a menu with more choices. Some frames have a subframe below with a scroll bar; scroll until you see the desired entry in the subframe; CL that entry and it will appear in the top frame as your choice. When a dialog panel is behind another panel CL the tab of the hidden panel to bring it to the front.

disk To access, CL Open, DBLCL the desired drive. **or** DBLCL My Computer, DBLCL the desired drive.

display appearance items The Color and Size of certain items and the Color, Size, and Font type for those items are set here. The items and what can be set are: 3D objects (such as buttons) **C**, active title bar (height) **CS** & **FCS**, active window border **CS**, applications background (inside of the MsWord window without a document) **C**, caption buttons **S**, desktop (color of the background for the onscreen icon titles and the dialog panel frames) **C**.
Other items and what can be set are: icons **S**, icon spacing horizontal **S**, icon spacing vertical **S**, inactive title bar **CS** & **FCS**, inactive window border **CS**, menu **CS** & **FCS**, message Box **CS** & **FCS**, palette title **S** & **FS**, scrollbar **S**, Selected items (you select them by clicking on them on the panel display) **CS,** tool tip **C** & **FCS**, and window **S** & **FS**.

display appearance items.. Change.
CL Start, RAO Settings, CL "Control Panel", DBLCL Display, CL Appearance tab. In the Item frame CL ▼. CL the item you want to change. To change a size CL the up/down arrows. To change a color CL the color arrow to view a color menu; CL the desired color. When you have the right size and color settings CL Apply. To leave the panel CL OK.

On the appearance panel if you can't
find the color you want: CL "Other" on
the color menu and a panel appears with
dozens of new colors and a beautiful
spectrum where you can create your own
color and add it to the custom color box
on this special panel.

Note: Sometimes the word "Other" on
the drop down color menu is hidden by
the taskbar; you may have to move
some things around to find it.

down arrow ▼   This small black
triangle appears on the right edge of
many panel frames. CL it and a list or
menu appears. See "List Box".

Drag with an arrow. Place the arrow on
the item to be dragged. CLHold the left
mouse button. Move the item to the new
location. Release the mouse button. To
drag a copy but leave the original:
PRHold the Ctrl key before dragging.

**Drag a window edge or corner to change
the window size or shape.** Place the
arrow tip on an edge or corner where
it will become a double-arrow. CLHold
and drag the edge or corner to the new
location. Release.

Drag hilited text. Move Ibby to the
start of the hilited text where it will
change into the arrow. (For a single

character hilite it takes some patience to find the spot where Ibby becomes the arrow.) CLHold and drag the item to the new location. Release.

drawings See Appendix 6 "Insert a Drawing or Photograph from the Clip Art Files." Also see Appendix 5 "Graphics". Also see "symbols, characters, and graphics.. Insert them into your document." under **S**.

drawings.. Create an original drawing with the help of the drawing program. CL the Drawing button on the Standard toolbar; the Drawing toolbar appears with tools for drawing lines and standard shapes, for rotating and positioning the shapes, for adding shadow and color etc.. See a bigger book for a complete description.

drives.. Access. CL Open, DBLCL the desired qdrive. **or** DBLCL My Computer, DBLCL the desired drive.

drop down lists These appear when you CL the down arrow. See "lists" under **L**.

e-mail (electronic mail) explained using AOL (American On Line)

First perform the following to save all outgoing and incoming messages in the "Personal Filing Cabinet":
While online, in the AOL Window
CL Members, CL Preferences, CL Mail.
CL to put check-marks in front of "Retain all mail I send in my Personal Filing Cabinet" and in front of "Retain all mail I read in my Personal Filing Cabinet".

e-mail.. Access new e-mail messages.
DBLCL the AOL icon, enter your password, CL "SIGN ON", **Wait.** CL "Mail Center", CL "Read New Mail".

e-mail.. Access old e-mail messages offline. DBLCL the AOL icon, CL File, CL "Personal Filing Cabinet". Scroll to and DBLCL the desired message.

e-mail.. Carry an e-mail message offline on the clipboard. While online place the arrow inside the message and CL it. CL Edit, CL "Select All", CL Edit again, CL Copy, CL the **X** at the top right corner of the monitor. **Wait.** DBLCL MsWord, CL Paste.

e-mail.. Delete "Headers" (routing data) from the end of an e-mail message before printing. See "Delete "Headers".." under D.

e-mail.. Save. See "Save an e-mail message in an offline folder while online."under **S**.

e-mail.. Send an e-mail message. Assuming that you want to compose the message offline: DBLCL the AOL icon on the Desktop. CL the "Pad and Pencil" icon on the AOL Toolbar. After "To:" type the e-mail address of addressee. PR Tab to send Blinky to "CC:". Type the e-mail address of any other recipients. PR Tab. Type a subject. PR Tab. Type your message. CL "Send Later". When told your message has been saved for later delivery CL OK. Enter your password, CL SIGN ON, **Wait**. CL the File Cabinet icon on the AOL Toolbar. DBLCL the icon of the letter you composed. The composing screen appears. CL Send.

emergency start-up disk As insurance against the time when your computer refuses to start you can create a floppy disk that may be of help in that event. CL Start, RAO Settings, CL Control Panel. DBLCL the "Add/Remove Programs" icon, CL the "StartUp Disk" tab, CL the "Create Disk" button. Insert a blank floppy disk into the drive. CL OK. WAIT. CL OK. Remove the floppy disk, mark it as the Emergency Start-up Disk and store it with your other disks.

E 3

Enlarge or reduce the size of an image.
If you want to enlarge an image and the
screen is too small to show the desired
size CL the Zoom arrow ▼ and CL 25%.
Bring the pointer inside the image and
it becomes a crossed double-arrow. CL
and eight tiny boxes surround the image.
Center the crossed double-arrow on the
lower right hand tiny box. It becomes a
tilted double-arrow. CLHold and the
tilted double-arrow becomes a precision
crossline.
Drag the corner down and to the right
until the rectangle fills the desired
area; release and the image fills that
area. (To reduce the size of the image
drag the corner up and to the left.)

Enlarge or reduce the size of a window.
Position the arrow point on the lower
right corner of window until it becomes
a tilted double arrow. Drag the corner
diagonally to change the window size.

**Enlarge or reduce the size of a symbol
or character.** Hilite the symbol or
character. In the font size frame CL ▼
and CL a larger or smaller font size.
CL the right margin. (A symbol, drawing,
or character in 48 point type is quite
impressive.)

envelopes.. Print an envelope with default settings. (To print an envelope with your own choice of fonts, etc. see Appendix 9.)
DBLCL MsWord, CL Tools, CL "Envelopes and Labels", CL the Envelopes tab. In the "Delivery address" frame type the name and address of the intended recipient. In the "Return address" frame, if your name and address aren't as you want them type the corrections. CL Options, CL the "Envelope Options" tab. In the "Envelope size" frame CL ▼, and scroll to and CL the desired envelope size. (The usual small envelope is "Size 6 3/4" and the usual business envelope is "Size 10".) CL OK. Insert an envelope into your printer feeder. CL Print. If the envelope was not printed properly See Appendix 9. For announcement-size envelopes that Windows says are too small see Appendix 11.

envelopes.. Print an envelope with default settings when you have a letter onscreen.
Hilite the adressee's name and address on the letter, CL Tools, CL "Envelopes and Labels", CL the Labels tab. The Delivery name and address appear in the Delivery address frame. In the "Return address" frame, if your name and address aren't as you want them type the corrections.
CL Options, CL the "Envelope Options" tab. In the "Envelope size" frame CL ▼, and scroll to and CL the desired envelope size. (The usual letter envelope is "Size 6 3/4" and the usual business envelope is "Size 10".) CL OK. Insert an envelope into your printer feeder. CL Print.
Note: Appendix 9 tells you what to do if the addresses were not properly oriented on the envelope. It also tells you how to print on announcement-size envelopes that Windows says are too small.

equal sign bold = On screen when you type an equal sign in bold it may not appear to be bold like the text around it. Don't worry; in print it will appear bold.

explorer See W'Explorer.

Fax a document from the computer.
It is much easier to use the fax machine directly, but if you don't want to do that see a bigger book for the directions.

file.. Change the name of a file.
With the file icon showing in its folder window RTCL the icon, CL Rename. Type a new name. PR Enter. Note: If the full name isn't accepted, put an empty space at the end of the first line and try again.

file.. Open a file. (same as Load a file.) DBLCL MsWord, CL Open. In the "Look in" frame CL ▼ . CL the drive the file may be on. DBLCL the folder it may be in, DBLCL the subfolder it may be in, etc. As soon as the file's icon appears in the large frame, DBLCL it and the file appears in the MSWord window.

files and folders   (organized confusion)
See page **F** 2.

files..Save in folders.
VITAL INFORMATION! See page **F** 3.

_____

_____

_____

_____

files and folders (organized confusion)
A difficult problem for a computer
novice is that common words are used
with different meanings.

In a non-computer office:

This is a letter or a memo.

This is a report or a document.

This is a photograph.

This is a file folder.

This is a filing cabinet. In a
non-computer office someone might place
the memo, letter, report, document and
photograph in a file folder. They might
open the drawer of a filing cabinet
where dozens of labelled "hanging file
folders" are supported by a "hanging
file folder frame". They might find the
hanging file folder with the proper
label and they might **file** the **file
folder** and its contents in it.

In a computer office:

These are all **files**.
They are **saved** in named **folders**
which are **saved** in other named **folders**
which are **saved** on a **hard drive** or **disk**.

files.. Save in folders.

Study these pages carefully; they will save you a lot of grief.

Assume you named a file "Bali" and you saved it in your "Travel" folder. When you open the "Bali" file you bring to the screen a <u>copy</u> of the "Bali" file; the original file stays in the "Travel" folder.

If you change the onscreen file in any way:
To <u>replace the original "Bali" file with the new version</u> CL File, CL "Save As". CL to put "Travel" in the "Save in" frame. "Bali" should be in the "File name" frame. CL Save. When asked "Do you want to replace the existing "Bali"? CL Yes."
To save the new version <u>and</u> retain the <u>original</u>. CL File, CL "Save As". CL to put "Travel" in the "Save in" frame. In the "File name" frame change the name (from "Bali" to "Bali 2", for example). CL Save. The "Travel" folder will now contain both the "Bali" and the "Bali 2" files.
<u>If you should happen to CL **X**</u> you will be asked "Do you want to save the changes you made to "Bali"". CL Cancel.

Files, continued

(If you CL No the new version will disappear and your new work will be lost.)

If you do not change the onscreen file in any way and you CL **X** the onscreen file disappears but the original "Bali" file remains in the "Travel" folder.

When you start work on a new file: After a few minutes work you should save (and name) the file. Further work can then be backed up automatically (See page **S** 1.) Otherwise you could CL **X**, CL No *and lose all your work*. If you happen to CL **X** immediately CL Cancel.

Find a lost folder or file. CL Start, RAO Find, CL "Files or Folders", type the name of the file, type the drive to be searched, CL "Find Now".

Find a "lost" window. Drag it by its title bar any other part into the open.

Find a specific word or phrase in a document. CL Edit, CL Find. Type the word or phrase in the "Find what" frame. CL "Find Next".

Find the lost taskbar. PR Ctrl+Esc.

floating toolbars A floating toolbar is a device for keeping a menu handy for repeated access. Such menus have a thin stripe across their top.

Explaining the floating toolbar:
Often when you CL an entry on a menu the menu disappears. Sometimes you would like to CL several entries. With some menus and sub-menus you can do that.
For example, CL Insert and then CL AutoText on the menu that appears.

A sub-menu titled AutoText appears with a thin stripe across the top that tells you it can "float". Place the arrow on the thin stripe, CLHold and drag the sub-menu away from the menu. The sub-menu becomes a floating toolbar.

Using the floating toolbar, for example:
On the AutoText floating toolbar
CL "All Entries", CL "Attention Line", CL Attention. The word "Attention:" appears on your document. CL "All Entries", CL "Ladies and Gentlemen". CL "All Entries", CL "Best Regards". You can quickly add the following (or similar words or phrases) to your document without typing a single word:
Attention:, ATTN:, Best regards, Cordially, Dear Sir or Madam, In Reply to, Ladies and Gentlemen:, REGISTERED MAIL, Subject: Via Facsimile, etc.

To remove the floating toolbar CL **X**.

F 6

Flow text around. See "Wrap text around"

folder.. Create a folder. CL Start,
CL Programs, CL W'Explorer. On the left
side CL the drive or folder you want
your new folder to be in. RTCL the right
side of window, CL New, CL Folder. Type
a name for the new Folder, PR Enter.
CL the right side of the window.

folders and files See "files and
folders".

folder.. Look inside. DBLCL on its icon.

**folders   Set up a group of useful
folders.**
The major folder should have your name
on it unless your name is very long.
"Bob's" or "Helen's", etc. makes a great
major folder. Install it on your hard
drive and also on your floppy or Zip
drive. Then into your major name folder
you might consider putting the following
sub-folders: Addresses, Auto, Business,
Charities, Condo, Daily, e-mail,
Finances, Forms, Health, Home,
Investments, Letters, Miscellaneous,
Music, Taxes, Sports, Travel and
Vacations. You will think of others.

font A type font is a set of characters
of a particular design. See "type fonts"
under **T**. Also see Appendix 4.

Format a new floppy disk. Don't. When you save (store) something on a new disk the program will guide you through the formatting.

format..Create pages that are high or wide. CL File, CL "Page Setup", CL the "Paper Size" tab, CL Portrait (for vertical) or Landscape (for horizontal).

_____
_____
_____
_____
_____
_____
_____
_____
_____
_____
_____
_____
_____
_____
_____
_____

G 1

games To access CL Start, CL Programs, CL Accessories, CL Games.

Give orders to the computer. See "Dialog panels".

graphics See "symbols, characters, and graphics" under **S**. Also see Appendix 4 "Type Fonts" and Appendix 5 "Graphics".

_____

_____

_____

_____

_____

_____

_____

_____

_____

_____

_____

_____

_____

_____

_____

_____

"Hilite" means to cover with a uniform color or density as when using a hilite pen. It is what computer people mean sometimes when they use the word "select".

Hilite a lot of text at the start of a document. Place Ibby where you want to end the hilite. CLHold and drag up and to the left until the pointer reaches the upper boundary of the screen; the hilited text will then fly by very quickly. When you reach the start of the document, release.

Hilite a lot of text at the end of a document. Place Ibby where you want to start the hilite. CLHold and drag down and to the right until the pointer reaches the lower boundary of the screen; the hilited text will then fly by very quickly. When you reach the end of the document, release.

Hilite an entire document. CL Edit, CL "Select All".

Hilite columns. Place Blinky at any corner of a column. PRHold Alt and CLHold and drag to the opposite corner. Release the ALT key and the mouse key.

Hilite in the Paint program.
CL "Select Tool", CLHold a place near the area, circle the area, return to initial place, release.

H ₂

Hilite quickly. To hilite <u>a word</u> DBLCL it. To hilite <u>a sentence</u> PRHold Ctrl and CL the sentence. To hilite <u>a paragraph</u> TripleCL it.

hilite.. Remove a hilite. CL the right margin (**or** PR Backspace **or** PR Delete).

Hilite text. With Ibby at one end of the text to be hilited CLHold and drag the black hilite to the other end, and release. Perform the next operation immediately.

Hilite text in color on the finished document (assuming you have a color printer). On the Hilite icon on the toolbar CL ▼. CL the desired color. (Note the tiny hilite pen on Ibby when he comes inside the text.) Hilite the text. Upon release of the mouse button the background is color hilited. To remove the color: hilite the text as before using the same color. To remove the highlight pen from Ibby PR back-space.If you have some tiny bit of color that can't be removed do the color highlight but CL None in the drop down color box.

hyphenate When you know where to put the hyphen place Blinky there, PR Ctrl + hyphen.

Hyphenate automatically as you type.
CL Tools, CL Language, CL Hyphenation.
CL to put a checkmark in the "Automatically hyphenate document" checkbox.The
"Hyphenation zone" frame controls the
maximum blank area at the end of a line;
leave it at .25" or CL your preference.
If you would prefer not to have more
than three hyphens in succession, for
example, CL to set the "Limit con-
secutive hyphens to" 3; if you don't
care how many successive hyphens there
are CL "No limit". CL OK.

To stop the automatic hyphenation:
CL Tools, CL Language, CL Hyphenation.
CLClear to remove the checkmark from the
"Automatically hyphenate document"
check-box. CL OK.

**Hyphenate..   Learn where to hyphenate
        a word when the Auto-hyphenate is
        off.**
Hilite the word. CL Tools, CL Language,
CL Hyphenation, CL Manual, CL Yes. If
that doesn't work CL Tools, CL Language,
CL Hyphenation, CL Manual. In the
"Hyphenate at" frame note the location
of the hyphens in the word and write
them on a note pad. CL Cancel. Place
Blinky where a hyphen should be,
PR Ctl+hyphen.

icons.. Arrange your icons. RTCL the folder window, CL Arrange Icons. For alphabetical arrangement, CL by Name. Otherwise CL by Type, Size, or Date.

icons.. Change the name of an icon (and its file). With the file icon showing in its folder window CL the icon, CL File, CL Rename. Type a new name. PR Enter.
Note: If the full name isn't accepted, put an empty space at the end of the first line and try again.

icons.. Change an icon's size, spacing, or background color. See "display appearance items" under **D**.

Increase/decrease the window size Point the arrow at the lower right corner of the window until the arrow becomes a tilted double arrow. Drag the corner to change the size of the window.

indents CL Format, CL Paragraph. In the "Indentation Left and Right" frames CL the desired amount. In the "Special" frame CL ▼ and CL either "(None)", or "First line" or "Hanging". If you chose "First line" or "Hanging" CL the arrows in the "By" frame to specify how much. To delete automatic indents: set the Left and Right frames to 0 and set the "Special" frame to (None). *Note that without automatic indents Blinky may* *"freeze" at the left edge of the text; PR Enter to unlock it.*

Insert a large capital letter at the start of a paragraph. See "Start a paragraph with a big fancy letter."

Insert a file in a document. Place Blinky where you want the file to be, CL Insert, CL File. On the "Insert File" panel in the "Look In" frame CL ▼. DBLCL the drive & DBLCL the folders until the icon of the wanted file appears. DBLCL that icon; the file is inserted automatically & you are returned to the document.

insert mode of typing In the <u>insert</u> mode when you begin typing in the middle of some text the text to the right keeps moving to the right. In the <u>overtype</u> mode the old text disappears. To switch between modes DBLCL the OVR button on taskbar. In the <u>insert</u> mode the letters OVR are very faint; in the <u>overtype</u> mode they are dark. If the OVR button is not available CL Tools, CL Options, CL the Edit tab, CL "Overtype mode" or CLClear to remove the checkmark from in front of "Overtype mode".

Insert text from document 1 into document 2. On document 1 hilite the text to be copied, CL Copy, CL X. Bring document 2 to the screen. Place Blinky. CL Paste.

Internet DBLCL the AOL icon or other network provider icon.

italics.. Type with italics. CL the *I* button on the toolbar and type. To stop typing with italics CL the *I* button again.
To add italics to existing text: hilite the text, CL the *I* button, CL the right margin.
To remove italics from existing text: hilite the text, CL the *I* button, CL the right margin.

---

joystick DBLCL MyComputer, DBLCL
       "Control Panel".

Justify   See "Align Text" under **A**.

_____

_____

_____

_____

_____

_____

_____

_____

_____

_____

_____

_____

_____

_____

_____

_____

_____

_____

keyboard, keystrokes.. Operate the computer by pressing keys.
All or almost all of the operations performed with a mouse can be done without the mouse. Sometimes using keystrokes will be much faster or more convenient than using the mouse.

Operating from the Menu Bar:
In Figure 1 note that on the Menu Bar (item 45) each of the button names has one underlined letter such as the F in File. If on the keyboard you PRHold Alt and PR F (or f) the File drop-down menu will appear as illustrated in Figure 3. Note the word Print on that menu. If you now PR P (or p) the Print panel appears. The general rule is PRHold Alt and PR the underlined letter on the menu button to display the drop-down menu. Then PR the underlined letter on a menu item.
Very useful keyboard commands:

COMMAND	KEYSTROKE
capitalization	Shift+F3 repeatedly
close window	Alt+F4
close all windows	Alt+F4 repeatedly
copy	Ctrl+C
cut	Ctrl+X
find	Ctrl+F
mail	Ctrl+M
new	Ctrl+N

COMMAND	KEYSTROKE
open	Ctrl+O
paste	Ctrl+V
print	Ctrl+P
save	Ctrl+S
select all	Ctrl+A
spell check	F7

Note: If you made a mistake, PR Ctrl+Z and the last thing you did on the computer will be cancelled.

Your favorite keyboard commands:

_____

_____

_____

_____

_____

_____

_____

_____

_____

_____

_____

Keyword on AOL To access an item quickly CL Keyword on the toolbar, type the name of the item, PR Enter.

L 1

labels Labels can be conveniently designed and printed using full page sheets of blank labels. Appendix 2 tells you how to create and save a reusable blank form for a given label size and then how to use it to create labels of that size.

layouts When typing a document there are five different layouts available: Normal, Online Layout, Page Layout, Outline, and Master Document. To choose one of the first four CL one of the layout buttons on the lower left of the MsWord window. If they are not there CL View, CL your choice of layout. For the Master Document layout CL View, CL Master Document.

The Normal layout has a ruler at the top of the page and a continuous blank "sheet" to type on. To indicate the end of a page and the beginning of the next page a horizontal dotted dividing line appears; that is the automatic page break.

The Online layout is for preparing online documents.

The Page layout has rulers at the top and at the left side of the page. It displays individual pages with their margins. When the text goes beyond the bottom margin of a page it is displayed just below the top margin of the next page. The Page layout is automatically set for certain procedures such as inserting a drawing or photograph from the Clip Art file into your document. <u>The Outline layout</u> and <u>The Master Document layout</u> are what they say they are.

letters See "Write a letter." under **W**.

line breaks Line breaks are used to solve some of the problems of the automatic formatting program. For more information see a bigger book. To eliminate some of the problems set the automatic indents to zero.
See "indents" under **I**.

line spacing.. Change the spacing between lines on existing text. Hilite the text. Then follow the procedure in the next paragraph.

line spacing when typing
CL Format, CL Paragraph, CL the "Indents and Spacing" tab. In the Spacing area in the "Line spacing" frame CL ▼ , CL 1, 1.5, or "double" space. For more line spaces CL "Multiple" and CL ▲ or ▼ in the "At" frame to set the desired number of line spaces.
You may also CL "Exactly" and then CL ▲ or ▼ in the "At" frame to set the desired number of points of line spaces. CL OK.

Add a little extra space above or below
a line of type in the single space mode.
CL Format, CL Paragraph, CL the "Indents
and Spacing" tab. To put space above the
line CL ▲ in the "Before" frame to set
the number of points. If the number you
want isn't shown, place Blinky in the
frame and type in the number of points.
The "After" frame puts space below the
line. CL OK.

Reduce the space between lines in the
single space mode. CL Format,
CL Paragraph, CL the "Indents and
Spacing" tab. In the Spacing area in the
"Line spacing" frame CL "Exactly" and
then in the "At" frame CL a few points
smaller than the type size. CL OK.
To resume normal typing: CL Format,
CL Paragraph, CL the "Indents and
Spacing" tab. In the Spacing area CL 0
in the Before and After frames and
CL "Single" in the "Line spacing" frame.
CL OK.

lists Lists appear when a frame down arrow ▼ is clicked. When the list is long sometimes you can type in the text box the first few letters of a desired word and the list will scroll automatically to the nearest word. Sometimes a scroll bar appears on the list; use it like a regular scroll bar. When a list entry is clicked it often appears also in the text frame.CL an open area to close a list or to close a menu. When it is permitted to choose more than one item from the list PRHold Ctrl and CL on each desired item.

list of open windows The list is on the taskbar.

Locate a file. CL Start, RAO Programs, CL W'Explorer, CL Folders until the file appears in the right hand column. Then DBLCL it.

Locate a specific word or phrase in a document. CL Edit, CL Find. Type the word or phrase in the "Find what" frame. CL "Find Next".

M 1

Make a mistake? PR Ctrl+Z.

Make a terrible mistake and everything freezes up? PR Ctrl+Alt+Delete.

margins CL File, CL "Page Setup". Set the margins by clicking the arrows. If you want a margin to be 1.25 but the arrows only go in steps of 1.2, 1.3 etc., insert Blinky in the frame, erase the setting and type in 1.25. CL OK. For most work the Gutter, Header and Footer can be set to 0.
If the margins were set below the program minimums a warning appears; CL Fix to show the minimums. To stay out of trouble set the margins for no less than: top 0.2, bottom 0.6, left 0.3, right 0.3.
When you attempt to print a document sometimes you will get the following abrupt note: "The margins of section 1 are set outside the printable area of the page. Do you want to continue?" If you have set the margins at or above the minimums suggested above CL Yes. Note that the default condition margins (what you get if you don't do something about it) wastes almost half of an 8 1/2 x 11 inch sheet of paper.

margins, normal or default settings
The program has chosen a particular type font, type size, margins setting, etc. for your use when starting a new document.

You may, of course, change any or all of these "default" settings at any time. However to have your choices appear automatically every time you start a new document, follow the procedure "Change the default settings for margins." under **C**. If that doesn't work see Appendix 8, "Change The Default Type Font and Margins."

Maximize or halve the window size. DBLCL the Title Bar. **or** CL the Maximize or Restore button. Note: When the window is full size the Maximize button turns into the Restore button.

[**Caution**: The Maximize button is very close to the Close **(X)** button.]

Minimize all windows. RTCL an open area of the task bar, CL "Minimize All Windows".

Mistakenly PR Alt? Press again. If that doesn't work PR Esc.

Mistakenly press several keys at once? PR Ctrl+Z.

monitor backgrounds (screen or desktop backgrounds) See wallpaper.

mouse pointers These are at first a tilted white arrow ↖, the point of which is used to Click on items or to Drag items.
When the arrow is in text it becomes Ibby I which is used to position (and when clicked on creates) Blinky | for typing. Ibby is also used to hilite text. It must be very close to a block of text before the arrow ↖ turns to I.
   When the arrow point is on an edge of a window it becomes ↔ or ↕ for dragging that edge to change the window's width or height (and sometimes to move it). When the arrow point is on the corner of a window it becomes a tilted double arrow for dragging the corner to change the window size.
 When it becomes an hourglass it means WAIT. An hourglass with an arrow means current work may be slowed by other work. Crossed double arrows can be used to move, enlarge or diminish a window. Other pointers include a circle with a slanted line inside ⊘ that tells you the pointer doesn't apply at that location, a fine cross line for precision movement, double lines with perpendic-ular double arrows that define the line between labels, etc.

mouse properties Change the properties and appearance of your mouse (and see some incredible variations). DBLCL MyComputer, DBLCL Control Panel, DBLCL Mouse. CL the Buttons tab and adjust the double-click speed. CL the Pointers tab. In the Scheme frame CL ▼, and CL an exotic design for the pointers. [To get back to normal CL ▼, CL (None).] CL the Motion tab to set the pointer motion speed and the length of the pointer trails. CL OK.

Move an image. Bring the pointer inside the image and it becomes a crossed double-arrow. CL and eight tiny squares appear. Move the double arrows to center on an edge (away from the tiny squares). CLHold and drag the image to where you want it.

Move the contents of the clipboard to a window. Place Blinky where you want the material to go, CL Paste.

Move the page up or down. To move the page a line at a time CL a scroll arrow. To move the page faster CLHold the arrow. To move an entire page CL a "double scroll arrow". To move quickly through a multi-page document drag the scroll box.

Move some text to a nearby location.
Hilite the text to be moved. Move Ibby
to the beginning of the hilite where he
becomes an arrow. Drag the hilite to the
desired location; a dotted insert line
shows where the text will be inserted.
Release. CL the right margin. Note: When
moving a single character it takes some
patience to get Ibby to turn into an
arrow. (To move a copy of the text and
leave the existing text intact PRHold
Ctrl before dragging.)

**move some text to a location not
currently visible onscreen.** Hilite the
text to be moved. CL Cut. Place Blinky
where you want the text to be placed.
CL Paste.

Move text from one document to another.
See "Copy text from Document 1 into
Document 2."

Move a window on the desktop.
CLHold the titlebar and drag.

Move a window to the front. CL on any
open area of the window, or CL on that
window's icon on the taskbar.

My Computer.. View its contents.
DBLCL its icon.

normal settings   The program has chosen a particular type font, type size, margins setting, etc. for your use when starting a new document. You may, of course, change any or all of these "default" settings at any <u>time</u>. However to have your choices appear automatically every time you start a new document you must change a parti- cular file in a particular way. See Appendix 8, "Change the 'blank document'".

_____

_____

_____

_____

_____

_____

_____

_____

_____

_____

_____

_____

_____

_____

_____

O 1

Open a file = Load a file = Bring the file to the screen. (When you "open" a file you are moving a copy of the file and its program from a drive to RAM and to the screen.)

Open a file from the desktop.
DBLCL your personal folder icon. DBLCL the appropriate folders until the icon of the wanted file appears. DBLCL that icon. (When too many icons in one window makes one hard to find, CL View, CL List.)

Open a file from the MsWord window.
CL the "Open" icon. In the "Look in" frame CL ▼ or CL the nearby folder with the "up one level arrow" to locate an appropriate drive or folder. DBLCL the drive and/or DBLCL the folders until the icon of the wanted file appears. DBLCL the icon. If the file isn't located repeat the procedure.

Open a file that is a picture or graphic.
Some files will not open with the procedure given above. So, with the MsWord window onscreen CL Insert, CL Picture, CL "From File". In the "Look in" frame CL ▼, find and CL the desired file. CL insert.

overtype mode of typing Existing text disappears as you type over it. (In the insert mode existing text moves to the right.) To change modes DBLCL the OVR button on the taskbar. In the insert mode the letters OVR are very faint; in the overtype mode they are darker. If the OVR button is not visible CL Tools, CL Options, CL the Edit tab, CL "Overtype mode" or CLClear to remove the checkmark from in front of "Overtype mode".

_____

_____

_____

_____

_____

_____

_____

_____

_____

_____

_____

_____

_____

P 1

page break, automatic The automatic page break is a horizontal dotted line that indicates the end of a page and the start of the next page on the continuous sheet of the "Normal View" layout.
In the "Page Layout" viewing mode separate pages are displayed. When the text runs beyond the bottom margin of page 1 it appears on page 2 below the top margin.

page break, manual In the "Normal View" layout if page 2 of a three page document is only half full of text, to come to the next automatic page break you would have to CL Enter too many times. Instead, when you reach the bottom of the text PR Ctrl+Enter and a dotted line with the words Page Break appears; this is the manual page break. Just below that dotted line page 3 will begin. <u>To remove a manual page break</u> backspace into it.

paper size.. Set the paper size.
CL File, CL "Page Setup", CL the "Paper Size" tab. In the "Paper Size" frame CL ▼, Scroll to and CL your paper size. CL Portrait for a vertical format or CL Landscape for a horizontal format. Note the image of your file in the Preview area. CL OK

paper, using it sideways To use a sheet of 8 1/2 x 11" paper sideways: CL file, CL "Page Setup", CL the "Paper Size" tab, CL Landscape. <u>To see the full width</u>: in the Zoom button frame CL ▼, CL "Page Width". <u>To print:</u> CL File, CL Print, CL Properties, CL Landscape, CL OK. Set the page range, number of copies, etc., CL OK.

paragraph button When you CL ¶ (the paragraph button) your document shows a dot between every word and a paragraph sign after each of what the program terms a paragraph. Some people find this helps in editing their document. Other people find it confusing. To learn more see a bigger book. To remove the dots and paragraph signs CL ¶ again.

⧄ **Paste** (Copy the contents of the clipboard onto a document.) Place Blinky where you want the contents to go. CL Paste. Note that the clipboard retains a copy of the contents for future use until a "cut" or "copy" command clears it to receive other contents.

photographs See Appendix 6.

pointer, mouse See "mouse pointer" under **M.**

P ₃

Print the clipboard onto the MsWord window. Position Blinky where you want the material to go. CL Paste.

Print a one page normal file. For one copy of one page in the Page Layout mode CL the Print button.

Print a wider-than-high file or a multi-page file. CL File, CL Print. To choose a vertical or horizontal format: In the upper right corner of the Print panel CL Properties. CL the Paper tab. CL Portrait for letters or CL Landscape for wide spreadsheets or for pictures of the screen.
To choose the desired print quality CL the Setup tab; CL Best or CL Normal or CL EconoFast. CL OK.
Back on the Print panel choose which pages you want to print. In the "Page Range" area: CL All; or CL "Current Page" (which is the page Blinky is on); or CL "Pages" and enter into the "Pages" frame the pages you want to print like 1,2,3,4 or 1-4
Choose the number of copies by Clicking the number in the Copies area.
CL if you want them collated or not.
For publishing: In the Print frame
CL ▼ , CL "All pages in range" or CL "Odd Pages" or CL "Even Pages". When satisfied CL OK and the printing begins.

Note 1. Assume the file you want to
print consists solely of pages 10, 11,
and 12 of some document. The numbers you
would insert into the "Pages" frame
would be 1,2,3 or 1-3. CAUTION: If you
put an extra comma after the 3 in 1,2,3
the program will not accept your order.
Note 2. On the Print panel in the lower
left corner is the Options button. If
you CL it you will see another panel
filled with complicated options. For a
full explanation see a bigger book.

**Print a picture of the screen. (Print
the desktop.)** CL New to get a blank
document. CL File, CL "Page Setup",
CL the "Paper size" tab, CL the "Paper
size", CL Land-scape. CL the Margins
tab. CL 0.6 margins all around and
CL 0 header and 0 footer. CL OK. PR the
PrintScreen key. (A picture of the
screen goes onto the clipboard.)
DBLCL MsWord. CL the "Normal View"
button. With Blinky in the blank
document CL Paste. Enlarge the image to
its maximum size in the window (See
"Enlarge an image." under **E.**). CL Print
etc. to print a copy. CL File, CL "Save
As", etc. to store the image for future
use.

Print an envelope. See "envelope.. Print an envelope.." under **E**. Also see Appendix 9.

print preview To see a small version of the page CL File, CL Print Preview. It is especially important to preview before you print when using graphics or when taking a picture of the screen because what you see on the screen is not always what you get when you print. To return to normal size CL File, CL Print Preview.

print quality.. Set the printer for best, normal or fastest. CL File, CL Print, CL Properties, CL the Setup tab. CL Best or CL Normal or CL EconoFast. CL OK. To return to the document CL Close or to print the document CL OK.

problems? See Appendix 1.

programs CL Start, RAO Programs. To see even more programs RAO Accessories. To put a program into operation CL it.

_____

_____

_____

_____

_____

quick view of a file
(seeing the contents of the file without bringing up its program) RTCL the icon. CL Quick View, CL the tiny Wdocument icon under File.

_____

_____

_____

_____

_____

_____

_____

_____

_____

_____

_____

_____

_____

_____

_____

_____

_____

_____

Reduce or enlarge a window. Position the arrow point on the lower right corner of the window until it becomes a tilted double arrow. Drag the corner diagonally to change the window size.

Remove & restore a window. To remove a window from the screen but keep it available CL the minimize button on the Toolbar; the window disappears and a titled button appears on the Taskbar. To restore it to the screen CL that button.

Remove a hilite. CL the Right Margin.

Rename a file or a folder (and its related icon). Bring the folder icon or the file icon to the screen. RTCL it, CL Rename, Type the new name in the frame, CL an open area.

Repeat a line or group of lines quickly. Hilite the line or lines, CL Copy. CL the right margin. CL Paste repeatedly until the page is full of lines. Use this method any time you want to repeat something quickly.

Replace a word with another word throughout a document. CL Edit, CL Replace. In the "Find what" frame type the word you want to replace. PR Tab. In the "Replace with" frame type the desired word. CL "Replace all". When a note appears telling you that the replacements have been made CL OK.

Replace existing type fonts.
Replace existing type fonts with
different or special fonts: hilite the
text, CL Format, CL Font, CL Font tab.
CL your choice in Font, Font Style,
Size, Underline & Color. CL any special
treatment in the Effects area of the
panel, CL OK. CL the Right Margin.

Retrieve a file from the recycle bin.
Place on the desktop an open folder
window into which you want the retrieved
file to go. DBLCL the Recycle Bin icon.
From the list that appears drag the
wanted file to the open folder window.

Save (backup) files automatically.
CL Tools, CL Options, CL the Save tab.
CL the "Always Create Backup Copy"
checkbox, CL the "Save AutoRecovery info
every" checkbox and CL in the number of
minutes between saves. CL OK.

Save a file (store it). CL File,
CL "Save As". In the "Save in" frame
CL the down arrow. CL your personal name
folder, DBLCL the folders and subfolders
until the folder in which you want to
save the file appears in the "Save In"
frame. If the desired name isn't in the
"File name" frame type it in. CL Save.
Also see page **F** 3.

**Save a file (store it) on a removable
disk.** With the document onscreen
CL File, CL "Save As". In the "Save In"
frame CL ▼ . CL the icon of the disk
(Floppy, Zip, Jaz), CL the folders until
the desired folder appears in the "Save
In" frame. If the desired name isn't
in the "File Name" frame type it in.
CL Save.

**Save an e-mail in an offline folder
while online.** While online CL File,
CL "Save As". In the "File name" frame
type a title. CL the icons until your
e-mail folder appears in the "Save in"
frame. CL Save.

scraps.. Leave them on the desktop.
Hilite the scraps, and drag them to
the desktop.

screen background See wallpaper.

screen saver RTCL Desktop,
CL Properties, CL the "Screen Saver"
tab. In the frame labeled "Screen
Saver" CL ▼ to display a menu of
patterns. CL a name and view the
pattern. CL Settings and try the various
options. CL OK. CL Preview to see the
Screen Saver pattern on the full screen
for a few seconds. At "Wait", set the
time after computer use before the
Screen Saver begins. You can also set
a time for the Low Power Standby or Shut
Off Monitor to begin. When you have the
right settings CL OK.

scroll arrows, vertical To move the
page a line at a time CL a scroll arrow.
To move the page faster CLHold a scroll
arrow. To move one window frame at a
time CL the scroll bar above or below
the scroll box. To move a page at a time
CL a double-arrow (Next Page or Previous
Page button). To move even faster see
"scroll box".

_____

_____

_____

scroll box, vertical To move quickly from one end of a multi-page document to the other drag the scroll box.

scroll box, horizontal When you have moved the horizontal scroll box to the extreme left and some text is still hidden CL the scroll arrow.

Scroll through the list in the frame of the Symbol dialog panel. CL Insert, CL Symbol. Place Ibby in the Font frame and CL. Use the up and down arrow keys to scroll through the list. Place the arrow on a character and CL; the image is enlarged. Use the arrow keys to move to any character to be enlarged.

Scroll through a list in the frame of a dialog panel a "page" at a time. (This is very useful when scrolling through type fonts.) On the frame CL ▼ and the scroll list appears. Read the first "page" of the list and then CL on the scroll bar below the scroll box; the next "page" appears. Repeat for the entire list.

shortcut.. Create a shortcut. To put the icon of an often-used item (program, folder, or file) on the desktop: DBLCL My Computer, DBLCL the drive that holds the desired item, DBLCL icons until the desired icon appears. RTDrag the icon to the Desktop. RTCL the icon, CL "Create Shortcut".

shortcut to oft-used symbols and characters
See Appendix 3.

Shrink a window. Point the arrow at the lower right corner of the window until the arrow becomes a tilted double arrow. Drag the corner to change the size of the window.

small letters (lower case)..Change to caps.
Hilite the text. PRHold Shift. PR F3 repeatedly to go from all caps to no caps to first caps. When satisfied CL the right margin.

sound properties window DBLCL MyComputer, DBLCL ControlPanel.

space between characters.. Change.
CL Format, CL Font, CL the "Character Spacing" tab. In the Spacing frame CL ▼, CL normal, expanded, or condensed. CL the amount of expansion or condens-ation in points in the By frame. You can view the effect in the Preview window. CL OK.

space between lines.. Set. See "line spacing" under **L**.

special type fonts See "type font, special" under **T**.

Spell-check a document. CL the ABC box on the Toolbar. When a "strange" word is found it appears in red. If it is a useful word that you want to keep in your personal dictionary CL Add, CL OK. To accept it this time CL Ignore. When told the spell-check is finished CL OK.

Spell-check as you type. This is a frustrating experience; wait until the document is finished and then use "Spell-check a document" above. To delete the automatic spell-check CL Tools, CL Options, CL "Spelling & grammar" tab. CL/Clear "Check spelling as you type", CL/clear "Check grammar as you type", and CL/clear "Check grammar with spelling". CL OK.

Spell-check a word.
Hilite the word. CL the ABC button. If a mistake is found you will be asked to correct it or ignore it.

spike This is a way to cut several items to the clipboard before pasting. (For example, if you want to move paragraphs 2, 4, and 7 to page 3.) Hilite the first item and PR Ctrl+F3. Repeat for the second item, etc. When you have collected the desired items on the clipboard place Blinky where you want the items and PR Ctrl+Shift+F3.

(For drawings and photos, instead of
hiliting each item CL on each item and
PR Ctrl+F3.)
If you have collected several items on
the clipboard using the spike and you
want to use the material online: Open a
blank document, PR Ctrl+Shift+F3 to put
the material on the blank document.
Hilite the material, CL Copy, CL **X**. Go
online and when you are composing your
letter place Blinky where you want the
material, CL Edit, CL Paste.

spreadsheets See appendix 10.

Start a paragraph with a big fancy
capital letter the easy way. Hilite the
first letter in the paragraph. In the
Font frame CL ▼, scroll to and CL a
fancy font, say Algerian. In the "Font
Size" frame CL ▼, scroll to and CL a
larger type size, say 36. CL the right
margin.

S **tart a paragraph the professional
way** (Create a Drop Capital Letter).
Place Blinky somewhere in the
paragraph. CL Format, CL "Drop
Cap". CL the "Dropped" frame. In the
Font frame CL ▼, scroll to and CL a fancy
font, say Lucinda Caligraphy.
In the "Lines to drop" CL the arrows to
set 3 or 4. In the "Distance from text"

frame CL the arrows to set 0.1 for
example. CL OK. CL the right margin.
Once you have the big letter you can
change its font, size, color, etc.:
DBLCL its invisible frame to hilite it.
Then CL any of the usual buttons,
including bold. CL the right margin. To
raise the letter a little hilite the
frame and drag it up.
**Note: To create the drop capital letter
MsWord switches to the "Page Layout
View". If you switch to "Normal View"
the Drop Cap effect seems to disappear.
It will still print properly. To prove
it: CL File, CL Print Preview.**
To remove a drop cap place Blinky
somewhere in the paragraph. CL Format,
CL "Drop Cap", CL the "None" frame,
CL OK.

Start with a big word: hilite
the word, CL Format, CL
"Drop Cap". CL the "Dropped" frame. In
the Font frame CL ▼, scroll to and CL a
fancy font. In the "Lines to drop" frame
CL the arrows to set 2 or 3, for example.
In the "Distance from text" frame CL the
arrows to set 0.1 for example. CL OK.
CL the right margin.
**Note: To start with a big word MsWord
switches to the "Page Layout View". If
you switch to "Normal View" the effect
seems to disappear. It will still print**

**properly. To prove it: CL File, CL Print
Preview.**
<u>To remove the big word</u> place Blinky
somewhere in the paragraph. CL Format,
CL "Drop Cap", CL the "None" frame,
CL OK.

**Store a document (Save a file) on the
main drive.** CL File, CL "Save As". In
the "Save in" frame CL ▼. DBLCL the
(C:) drive, DBLCL the folders and the
subfolders until the folder you want to
save the file in appears in the "Save In"
frame. If the desired name isn't in the
"File name" frame type it in.
CL Save.

**Store a document (Save a file) on a
removable disk.** With the document on
screen CL File, CL "Save As". In the
"Save In" frame CL ▼. CL the icon of
the disk (Floppy, Zip, Jaz), CL the
folders until the desired folder appears
in the "Save In" frame. If the desired
name isn't in the "File Name" frame type
it in. CL Save.

symbols, characters & graphics.. Insert.
(Type font characters and symbols are
shown in Appendix 4, Graphics in

Appendix 5. See Appendix 3
for a quick way to produce
oft-used symbols and characters. Also see "Text

Boxes" in Appendix 7 and "Wrap text around a drawing or picture." under **W**.) You can insert into your documents a variety of characters and symbols that do not appear on your keyboard, as well as graphics (drawings). There are thousands of these items on the symbols panels and on the character maps. They can be enlarged in your document using the font size button to add an artistic and professional look to your work. There are two places where these items can be found, each with certain advantages. The two procedures are significantly different.

Note: For most inserts MsWord switches to the "Page Layout View". If you switch to "Normal View" the effect seems to disappear. It will still print properly. To prove it: CL File, CL Print Preview.

symbols.. the symbols panels
Set the font size to 16 so the symbols will be big enough to see clearly. Place Blinky where you want the symbol, character, or graphic to go. CL Insert, CL Symbol, CL the Symbols tab. In the Font frame CL ▼ and a long scroll list of font types appears.
CL a font name and a panel appears with hundreds of little boxes containing all the symbols, characters, and graphics available in that type font. To enlarge a box to see it more clearly CL it.

To insert a symbol into your document:
CL it; on the bottom of the panel CL the
Insert button. The symbol has been
inserted into your document. If desired
CL another symbol, CL the Insert button,
etc. CL the "Special Characters" tab.
CL a character, CL the Insert button,
etc. When finished CL Cancel. All of the
symbols are on your document near
Blinky.

symbols..the Character Map
CL start, CL Programs, CL Accessories,
CL "Character Map". On the Font frame
CL ▼ and a very long scroll list
appears with True Type fonts. CL a font
name and its character map appears with
hundreds of little boxes with all the
characters, symbols, and graphics that
are available in that type font. To see
an enlarged image CLHold the desired
box.
To insert one or more characters into
your document: CL a character,
CL Select; that character appears in
the "Characters to copy" frame. Repeat
with another character if desired. When
you have enough characters CL Copy,
CL Close.
Place Blinky where you want the
characters to appear, CL Paste and the
characters appear on your document.

(The size of the graphics from the
character map when first inserted
onscreen is always 12 point, regardless
of the setting of the font size button.
To enlarge them see "Enlarge or reduce
the size of a symbol or character" under
E.)
Note: Some day when you have a spare
hour explore all the boxes on all the
panels for all of the type fonts on the
Symbols panel and on the Character Map.
You will be amazed at the variety of
characters, symbols, and graphics that
are available.
(Or study Appendix 4 "Type Fonts" and
Appendix 5 "Graphics".)

symbols and characters by the numbers
  (See Appendix 3.)
For often-used symbols and characters
that do not appear on your keyboard
there is a quick method for bringing
them up. It requires you to know the
type font and special keystroke codes
for each symbol or character.

To understand how to get the codes for
symbols by the numbers:
CL start, CL Programs, CL Accessories.
CL "Character Map". In the Font frame
CL ▼ and use the scroll box to scroll
to the end of the long list of type
fonts. CL Wingdings (not Wingdings 2 or
Wingdings 3). In the bottom row of
symbols, the 11th from the right edge,
CL the tilted arrow to hilite it.

Note in the lower right hand corner
there is a button reading Keystroke:
Alt+0245. It means that when you are
typing and you want to insert the tilted
arrow use the procedure described in
Appendix 3 with Wingdings as the font
and ALT+0245 as the keystrokes.
Appendix 3 gives you the fonts and keystrokes for a number of the symbols used
in this book; it also has space where
you can insert your own often-used
symbols.

synonyms To find a synonym for a word
in the text hilite the word, CL Tools,
CL Language, CL Thesaurus.

tables.. Create forms, fill them in, and have them calculate for you.
        (See Appendix 10.)

tabs To set CL Format, CL Tabs.

taskbar The taskbar contains the Start button, a button for each open window, the clock, and several small but inter-esting icons. See Figures 1 & 2 for a description of each of them. You can also get a description of most buttons by resting the arrow tip on them.

templates A template is basically a pattern. Paper patterns for sewing are templates. A cookie cutter is a template. In the computer world a template is a particular selection (pattern) of document elements that is chosen for you (or that you choose) to get you started when you create a document. These elements include type font, font size, margins, document style, etc..
To see the icons of more than two dozen templates CL Start, CL "New Office Docu-ment", CL the Templates tab. Included are templates for a Fax, a Letter, a Memo, and a Resumé each in either Contemporary, Elegant or Professional style. An E-mail template is also provided. DBLCL an icon to bring the template to the screen and follow the directions to create your document.

The Templates panel also includes <u>Colorful stationery</u> (Flame, Rain, Midnight, Ocean, Height, and Urgent), <u>and Wizards</u> (helpful guides) for Envelopes, Letters, Labels, Fax, Memos, and Resumés.
For even more templates CL "More Templates and Wizards" and follow the directions. When you have used a template and changed it to suit your taste you should save it with a distinctive name like "Letter B" for business letter so you can find it easily for future use.

text box, defined (See Appendix 7.)
A text box is a rectangle into which you can insert text, drawings, work-sheets, photographs, tables, and other objects. You can change the size, shape, and location of the text box. You can control the inside contents of the text box and you can control how text wraps around the box.
You can change the border and add shading and 3D effects. You can change the direction of text inside the box and link boxes so that text flows from one box to another.

time, day, date.. Set. DBLCL the taskbar clock, CL the correct date on the calendar, CL ▼ on the month box, CL the correct month, CL the up or down arrows to correct the year. PR Tab until the hour in the time box is hilited, erase the old hour and type in the correct hour. PR Tab, set the minutes one minute fast. PR Tab, set the seconds to zero, PR Tab, set AM or PM. When the time is exact CL OK.

time, day, date.. View. DBLCL the taskbar clock.

time zone, daylight savings, auto adjust RTCL the taskbar clock, CL Adjust Date/ Time. CL the "Time Zone" tab, CL ▼ , CL the correct time zone, CL to put a checkmark in "Automatically adjusts for daylight savings changes". CL OK.

titlebar The titlebar is the top strip of a window. To move the window CLHold an open area on the title bar and drag it. The title bar displays the name of the program & the name of a contained file. It is lit up when it is the active window on the Deskpad. It holds the minimize, maximize, and **X** (close) buttons. CL the minimize button to turn the window into a small button on the Taskbar; to bring it back CL that button. To expand the window to fill the entire screen CL the maximize

button; it turns into a restore button
which does just that if clicked.

toolbar.. Add one. RTCL any toolbar. A
list of other toolbars appears. CL the
desired toolbar name. The new toolbar
will appear somewhere on desktop. Drag
it to the other toolbars and hide its
title bar to save space.
To delete a toolbar drag it by its
handle (the ridges on the far left)
until its title bar shows and CL **X**.

toolbar, defined (See Notes) Tool bars
are groups of icon buttons that are
positioned below the Menu bar. They are
shortcuts to program operations such as
Cut, Copy, Paste, Bold, Italics, Underlining etc.. When the instructions in
this manual say CL Cut, CL Copy,
CL Paste, etc. they are referring to the
buttons on the tool bars.

toolbars, floating See "floating
                        toolbars" under **F**.

trouble shooting See Appendix 1
                    "Problems?"

Turn off the AutoCorrection. If you
have problems with any of the automatic
parts of the program you can turn it
off. CL Tools, CL Autocorrect, CL the
Autocorrect tab. CLClear to remove the
checkmarks from any or all of the five
automatic boxes. CL OK.

Type a letter. See "Write a letter."
under **W**.

type font A type font is a set of characters of a particular design. Appendix 4
displays over 100 available type fonts.

**type font.. Change a font in existing
text.** See "type font, Replace" under **T**.

type font.. Choose from the toolbar.
In the Font frame CL ▼ , scroll to and
CL a font name. In the "Font Size" frame
CL ▼ , scroll to and CL a font size. CL
B for bold, CL *I* for italic, CL <u>U</u> for
underlined. CL the <u>A</u> down arrow ▼ for
font color and CL a color. Type with
your new type font.

type font graphics   See Appendix 5.

type fonts, normal The program has
chosen a particular type font, type
size, margins setting, etc. for your use
when starting a new document. You may,
of course, change any or all of these
"default" settings at any time.) However
to have your choices appear automatically every time you start a new document
follow the procedure "Change the default
settings for margins." under **C**. If that
doesn't work see Appendix 8.

type fonts.. Preview as you choose.
Choose a type font by seeing what they
actually look like. First see Appendix 4
where more than 100 available fonts are
displayed. Then to see a particular type
font on your screen: CL Format, CL Font,
CL the Font tab. In the Font frame
scroll to and CL a font name. In the
"Font style" frame CL a font style.
In the "Size" frame scroll to and CL a
size. In the Preview Window you can see
what your selection looks like. On this
panel you can also choose and preview
special fonts under "Effects". (See
below.) When satisfied CL OK. Type with
your new type font.

type font, special To type with
~~strikethrough~~, ~~double strike-
through~~, superscript , subscript,
shadow, outline, emboss,
engrave, SMALL CAPS, ALL CAPS, or
hidden: CL Format, CL Font,
CL FontTab, CL choice under "Effects".
CL OK.

**type font.. Remove a special font from
existing text.** Hilite the text,
CL Format, CL Font, CL FontTab, CLClear
the checkmarks under "Effects". CL OK.
CL the right margin.

type font.. Replace the font in existing text. Hilite the text. See "type font, Choose from the toolbar."; make your choices, CL the right margin.

typing mode, insert or overtype
When the letters "OVR" on the OVR button on the taskbar are very faint you are in the insert mode where typing moves existing text to the right. DBLCL the OVR button and the letters "OVR" become darker; you are now in the overtype mode where typing removes existing text. DBLCL the OVR button to change again.If the OVR button isn't available CL Tools, CL Options, CL the Edit tab, CL "Overtype mode" or CLClear to remove the checkmark from in front of "Overtype mode".

Type with wraparound. When the right margin is reached when typing, the program takes the first word that cannot fit on that line and puts it on the next line. If that leaves too large a gap see "hyphenate" under **H.**

Undo: RTCL the Desktop.

underlined type To type with underlin-
ing CL U on the toolbar and type.
To stop underlining while typing CL U.
Add underlines to existing text:
Hilite it, CL U, CL the right margin.
Remove underlines from existing text:
Hilite it, CL U, CL the right margin.

underlined type, special kinds There
are nine kinds of underlining in Word
97, fewer in earlier versions. The nine
types are single line, words only,
double, dotted, thick, dashes, dot dash,
dot dot dash, and wave.
The use of single line underlining has
been described above. The others are
used in a similar way except that
instead of "CL U" (on the formatting
toolbar) one must go to the Font panel.
To type with a special underlining:
CL Format, CL Font. In the Underline
frame CL ▼ , CL a title, CL OK. Type.
To stop typing with the special
underlining CL Format, CL Font. In the
Underline frame CL ▼ , CL (none), CL
OK.
To add special underlining to existing
text: hilite the text, CL Format,
CL Font. In the Underline frame CL ▼ ,
CL a title, CL OK, CL the right margin.
To remove special underlining from
existing text: hilite the text,

U 2

CL Format, CL Font. In the Underline frame CL ▼ , CL (none), CL OK, CL the right margin.

upper case (capital letters) Hilite the text. PRHold Shift. PR F3 repeatedly to go from all caps to no caps to first caps. When satisfied CL the right margin.

W 1

wallpaper.. Choose the background for the desktop. Remove all the windows from the Desktop for best viewing. RTCL the Desktop. CL Properties. (If the Properties button doesn't appear RTCL higher on the Desktop, then CL Properties.) Move the Properties dialog panel to the left side of screen for best viewing. CL the Background tab. Click Tile to put a dot in the circle. In the wallpaper frame CL the name of a sample to see it displayed on the small monitor. CL Apply to see it displayed on the Desktop. (Sometimes the dialog panel is so tall that the Apply button near its bottom is covered; if so lower the taskbar and raise the dialog panel.) Repeat for each of the samples. If you find the wallpaper sample that you want CL OK.

wallpaper.. Put a frame around it.
RTCL the Desktop, CL Properties, CL Center. In the Pattern frame CL (None). In the Wallpaper frame CL each of the wallpaper samples to see its size within the frame in the center mode (some of the samples show only a tiny bit of wallpaper in a huge frame). When you find an acceptable combination of wallpaper and size, CL an entry in the Pattern frame to see what that frame looks like surrounding the wallpaper. CL Apply to see what it looks like on the Desktop.

CL another entry in the Pattern frame, etc.. If you find a desirable combination CL OK. If you decide you don't want a frame at all CL Tile, CL OK. (To see a highly magnified image of the pattern for editing CL "Edit Pattern"; to go on to another pattern CL Done. CAUTION: If you CL Remove instead of Done you delete the pattern from the computer! If asked if you wanted to delete the pattern CL No. When you CL OK to exit, the background you see will remain.

wide documents When a document is wider than it is long (such as a spreadsheet or a picture of the screen) use the landscape mode to edit and print it. CL File, CL "Page Setup", CL the "Paper Size" tab, CL Landscape. Note that the Preview window shows the change in orientation and the width and height dimensions are interchanged. In the "Apply to" window CL the down arrow and CL either "This section", "This point forward", or "Whole Document". CL OK. When printing the document make sure that the Properties panel is set for Landscape.

wiggly underlines They indicate a misspelled or non-standard word. See Spell-check above.

W'Explorer CL Start, RO Programs, move right, CL Windows Explorer.

window.. Change its size. Point the arrow at the lower right corner of the window until the arrow becomes a tilted double arrow. Drag the corner to change the size of the window.

window.. Close it. CL **X**.

window.. Maximize its size. To fill the entire screen DBLCL the title bar. The Maximize button turns into the Restore button. To restore the original size DBLCL the titlebar. [CAUTION: The Maximize button is very close to the Close (**X**) button.]

window.. Move it on the desktop. CLHold the titlebar and drag it to where you want it.

window.. Move it to the front. CL on any open area of the window, or CL on that window's icon on the taskbar.

window.. Remove it & later restore it. To remove a window from the screen but keep it available CL the minimize button on the toolbar; the window disappears and a titled button appears on the taskbar. To restore it to the screen CL that button.

window.. Reduce the maximized size. DBLCL the titlebar.

window.. Shrink it to taskbar. CL the Minimize button on title bar. To restore CL the window's button on the taskbar.

windows.. Arrange them. RTCL the Clock. CL Cascade, or CL Tile Horizontally, or CL Tile Vertically.

windows A list of open windows is on taskbar.

windows.. Minimize all of them. RTCL the open area of the task bar, CL "Minimize All Windows". To restore CL each window button on task bar.

Word Art
Place Blinky where you want the WordArt (you can move it later if you wish). CL Insert, CL Picture, CL WordArt, CL the desired design, CL OK. In the Font frame CL ▼, scroll to and CL the desired font. In the Size frame CL ▼, scroll to and CL the desired size. If you want Bold or Italic CL them. Type the text, CL OK. The WordArt is inserted into your document, a WordArt command is added to the Format menu, and the Word-Art toolbar appears, allowing the design to be changed in a number of ways. For further details see a bigger book.

W 5

Wrap text around a drawing or photograph.

(See Appendix 6 "Insert a Drawing or Photograph".) CL the drawing, CL Format, CL Picture. On the "Format Picture" panel CL the Wrapping tab, CL Square, CL Right. In the "Distance from the text" area CL 0" for top, bottom and left and CL 0.1" for right. CL OK. If the drawing is not in the desired position bring the arrow over the drawing until crossed double arrows appear. CLHold and drag the drawing to the desired place. CL the right Margin.

Wrap text around a type font graphic.

(See Appendix 7 "Text Boxes".) Before you can wrap text around a type font graphic (as opposed to a drawing or photograph) you have to put a "text box" around it. Create the Text Box: Hilite the graphic. CL Format. CL "Insert Text Box". A text box appears surrounding the graphic. CL inside the frame and eight tiny boxes and a shadow frame appear. Move Ibby to the right bottom tiny box until the tilted double arrow appears. CLHold and drag the corner to size the text box to the graphic. Unlike a drawing or photo, to change the size of a type font graphic hilite it. In the Font Size frame CL ▼, CL a larger or smaller font

size. CL the right margin. (A symbol
in 48 point type is quite impressive.)
Prepare the box to be wrapped around:
CL inside the box, CL Format, CL Text
Box. On the "Format Text Box" panel
CL the Wrap-ping tab, CL Square,
CL Right. In the "Dis-tance from the
text" area CL 0" for top, bottom and
left and CL 0.1" for right. CL OK.
If the drawing is not in the desired
position bring the arrow over the box
frame until crossed double arrows
appear. CLHold and drag the drawing to
the desired place. CL the right Margin.

**Write a letter, but first create your
personalized stationery.** CL MsWord and
the composing window appears. CL File,
CL "Page Setup", WAIT. CL the "Paper
Size" tab. In the "Paper Size" frame
CL the down arrow, CL the size of your
paper. CL Portrait. [The Landscape mode
(long direction across) is used for
spreadsheets, signs, maps, etc..] Note
that the icon and the preview window
illustrate your choice. CL the Margins
tab. If what is shown is acceptable
CL OK. If not CL the up/down arrows
to set your choice. Let Gutter, Header,
and Footer be zero. CL OK.

_____

_____

_____

<u>Type a letterhead</u> with your name, or
name, address, phone, fax, e-mail etc.
Hilite the entire letterhead. To
increase the size of the type CL the
"Type size" down arrow and click 16 for
example. To change to Bold CL Bold. To
change to Italic CL Italic. To center
the letterhead CL the Center button on
the toolbar. When satisfied CL the right
margin. To change the size of the type
for the body of the letter CL the "Type
size" down arrow, etc.
<u>Before you type your first letter</u> you
may want to save this form for future
use, using the name "Letter form" or
something simple like that. See "Save a
file". (To save a second letter form for
a different size stationery name it
"Letter form 2".)

Write a letter. DBLCL "My Computer",
DBLCL the drive, folders, and subfolders
until your letter form icon appears.
DBLCL it. Type your letter.
<u>To put more space between the lines</u>:
hilite the text, CL Format, CL Paragraph. In the "Line spacing" frame
CL ▼ , CL 1.5 lines or CL double, CL OK.
<u>To make the main body of your letter</u>
<u>line up on both the left and the right</u>
<u>side</u>: hilite the text, CL the Justify
button on the toolbar. CL the right
margin. <u>To save the letter</u> see "Save a
file." under **S**. To print the letter see
"Print a file." under **P.**

Zoom button (See your work smaller or bigger.) In the zoom button frame (75% for example) CL ▼. The menu shows that you can enlarge up to 500% or diminish down to 10%. It also allows you to display the full width of your page. In the "Page Layout" mode when you

CL ▼ on the zoom button there are two more settings on the menu: Whole Page and Two Pages. These show you the overall look of a full page or two full pages.
Evidently the 100% setting was based upon a certain screen size. If you have a 16 inch diagonal viewing area on your screen your document will be close to full size at the 50% setting; at that setting 12 point type is difficult to read. There may be a way in the program for setting the 100% for a given screen size but the author hasn't found it.

_____

_____

_____

_____

_____

_____

_____

_____

Appendix 1   Problems?

alignment   The left margin is not aligned with the left edge of the window.   CL the horizontal scroll bar to the right of the scroll box and then CL it to the left of the scroll box.

Arrows ▼ and ▲ won't let you make a setting below a certain value or at a precise value.
When setting the line spacing (see line spacing under **L**) you may want the space on top of a line to be 2 points but when you CL ▲ the value goes to 6 points. Insert Blinky in the frame to the right of the 6, erase the 6 and type in 2. Also when setting margins, you may want a margin to be 1.25 but the arrows only go in steps of 1.1, 1.2, 1.3 etc.. Insert Blinky in the frame, erase the setting and type in 1.25.

Blinky won't move to the next frame when filling out forms?   PR the Tab key to move Blinky to the next frame, or move Ibby to the next frame and CL to produce Blinky.

Backspace won't work? PR Ctrl+Backspace.

Blinky "frozen" on the left edge of the text?   PR Enter to unlock.

Clicked top/right X but the window didn't disappear?   Remove the menu or other panel from the screen and try again.

Clicked top/right X but the window takes between 15 and 38 seconds to disappear. Sometimes this problem is caused by having saved too many pictures on the hard drive. Copy your pictures on a Floppy disc or Zip disc. Check to see they have transferred properly. Then delete the pictures from your hard drive and the problem may be solved.

Computer won't start? Remove the Floppy Disk from the drive. Wait a few seconds, try again.

Computer has slowed down. CL Start, CL Programs, CL Accessories, CL System Tools, CL Defragmenter. If that doesn't work move any photographs you have saved on your hard drive to a Zip disc or to Floppy discs.

Dialog panel bottom disappeared behind the taskbar. Drag the taskbar down, drag the dialog panel up.

Document refuses to be edited?
Create an editable copy.
Method 1. Hilite the entire text,
CL Copy, CL **X.** DBLCL Ms Word, CL New Document. CL Paste. If that doesn't work try:
Method 2. Scan a hard copy of the document with an OCR (optical character recognition for editing) scan program.

Document is too wide for the screen?
In the Zoom button frame CL ▼, CL 75%
or 50%. To use 8 1/2 x 11" paper
sideways CL File, CL Page Setup, CL the
"Paper Size" tab, CL Landscape. In the
Zoom button frame CL ▼ , CL 50%.

**Everything freezes & the mouse clicker
wont click.** PR Enter. If that doesn't
work PR Ctrl+Alt+Delete. If that doesn't
work and you have to press them again
you will lose whatever you were working
on. That's why it is a good idea to
automatically backup your work every ten
minutes. See Backup Files Automatically
under **B**.

indentation problems   For unwanted
indentations: hilite the entire area,
CL Format, CL Paragraph, CL the "Indent
and spacing" tab. In the Indentation
area in the Special frame CL ▼ ,
CL (none). CL OK.

Layout buttons disappeared: CL View.

**Message appears when you are trying to
open a file:** "Do you want to revert to
the saved "Letter to Mother"? YES or
NO." You don't know what to do because
you believe that all your files have
been saved and you don't know what the
message means.
It means (and it should say) that you
already have that file open and you

don't know it because it has been
minimized to a button or icon on the
taskbar or is hiding behine another
file. If you have made changes to the
minimized version of the file CL NO.
Bring the minimized file back to full
size: CL the button or icon and proceed
from there.

misalignment   You have used different
sizes of type or graphics in a line and
a vertical line of characters is
staggered as a result. Hilite several
spaces in front of the misaligned
character and change their size: In the
Font size frame CL ▼ , CL a smaller or
larger size until the character lines
up. Repeat with adjacent lines.

Nothing works. PR Enter. If that doesn't
work PR Ctrl+Alt+Delete.

OVR button disappears. You want to type
in the Overtype mode (where new typing
removes the existing type) but the OVR
button has disappeared. CL Tools,
CL Options, CL the Edit tab,
CL "Overtype mode", CL OK.
To return to the Insert mode (where new
typing moves existing text to the right)
CL Tools, CL Options, CL the Edit tab,
CLClear "Overtype mode", CL OK.

The printer won't work. CL Start, CL Settings, CL Printers, RTCL your printer. There should be no checkmark in front of "Pause Printing". There should be a checkmark in front of "Set As Default".

The right Ctrl button is always in the way?
Do you keep pressing the right Ctrl button when you are trying to press the right shift button, thereby causing horrible things to happen to your work? The author solved the problem by removing the button from the keyboard. He slipped the rounded tip of a table knife between the key and the top skin of the keyboard and gently pried the button until it pulled off.
He covered up the small cylinder that rose from the "floor" of the keyboard with a 1/2" diameter plastic pipe end protector. He still has the left Ctrl button which he doesn't usually hit inadvertently because the left Shift button is closer to the normal position of the left little finger than the right shift button is to the normal position of the right little finger.

Shortcut won't create in the folder.
When asked "Would you like to have a shortcut placed on the desktop?" CL Yes.

Space bar won't work when Blinky is at the left margin. PR Enter then PR the space bar.

A space refuses to be filled.
CL Format, CL Paragraph and see whether some strange setting has appeared in the indent frames, etc.. If so, remove it. If that doesn't work, create a text box in the space, then delete the text box. The space often behaves. See Appendix 7.

Strange things are happening. You have backspaced and the automatic program has changed your font, your font size, your non-bold setting, etc.etc.etc. Do whatever backspacing you must do and then change all of these setting back to what <u>you</u> want.

Taskbar disappeared. Use the monitor's up/down buttons to raise the display.

Text disappears to the left during a wraparound. PR Enter.

Toolbar disappeared. See "toolbar, add one" under **T**.

The Word program isn't working properly.
Have someone check to see how many programs are on your start-up routine. Having too many may alter your programs. Have someone remove the lesser used programs from your startup and reinstall all your programs.

Appendix 2 Labels

Create and save a form for a particular size label. (Once you have created and saved a form for a particular sized label the process for printing labels of that size is very simple, even though describing it is not simple.)
For clarity the description will use Avery Standard labels #8162 (1.33" high by 4" long, 14 to a sheet).
DBLCL MsWord, CL Tools, CL "Envelopes & Labels", CL the Labels tab, CL Options. To describe your printer CL "Laser & Ink Jet" or CL "Dot Matrix". In the "Label Products" frame CL ▼,
CL Avery Standard. In the Product Number frame scroll to and
CL # 8162 - address. CL OK. In the Print area CL "Full page of the same label" **even if you plan to print only one or a few labels.** CL "New Document". PR Space Bar, CL View, CL "Page Layout" and the rulers are laid out exactly like the sheet of blank labels with Blinky in the upper left label.
To save the form CL File, CL "Save As". In the "File Name" frame type "Label Form 1.33x4". In the "Save In" frame CL ▼, CL the drive and DBLCL the folders until the folder where you want to store the form is displayed in the frame. CL Save.

_____

_____

_____

_____

Create a single label on a sheet of blank labels with some of the labels gone.
Locate and bring to the screen the label form you created (see above) for the size label you want to create. Place Blinky in the first available label space. CL the font, font size, Bold, etc. as usual.
Type the label you want to create (It fills from the middle line.) If you type beyond the label boundaries the type disappears.
When you have the desired label check its fit into the label space: slowly move the arrow tip away from the left edge of the text; a double line/double arrow appears;
CL and a dotted line shows the edge of the blank label. Leave some left and right margin. If you want all the text but it doesn't fit change to a smaller type size. **When ready to print** insert a sheet of used paper in the printer and CL Print. Check the results. If you have put the text in the wrong label space move it to the correct space: hilite it, CL Cut, Place Blinky in the correct space, CL Paste.
When satisfied insert the partial sheet of labels in the printer. CL Print.

Create a second identical label.
Hilite the text of the first label. CL Copy, Place Blinky in the second label space, CL Paste. When ready

insert a sheet of used paper in the printer and CL Print. When satisfied insert the partial sheet of labels into the printer. CL Print.

Create a different second label. Place Blinky in that label space, type, etc. When ready insert a sheet of used paper in the printer and CL Print. When satisfied insert the sheet of partially used blank labels in the printer and CL Print.

Create a sheet of identical labels
Follow the directions to create a single label in the upper left label space. Hilite the label, CL Copy, place Blinky in the second label space, CL Paste. Place Blinky in the next empty space, etc. until the top row is filled. Hilite the top row, CL Copy. Place Blinky in row 2, CL Paste. Place Blinky in row 3, CL Paste, etc. until the page is filled. If the labels overflow onto the second page remove the excess: hilite, CL Cut. When ready insert a sheet of used paper in the printer and CL Print. When satisfied insert the full sheet of blank labels in the printer and CL Print.

_____

_____

_____

_____

_____

Appendix 3 Symbols & Characters by the numbers

Insert a symbol into your text quickly when you know its font and code number.

Place Blinky where you want the symbol to be. PR the "Numbers Lock" key (its light goes on). In the Font frame CL the down arrow ▼. Scroll to and CL the listed Font name. PR the listed key or keys. Repeat as desired.

To exit PR the "Numbers Lock" key (its light goes out), CL the Font frame down arrow ▼, CL your normal font.

for this symbol	CL this font name,	PR this or these keys
↰	Wingdings	PRAlt+0245
☑	Wingdings 2	PR R
⊙	Wingdings 2	PR 8
⊘	Wingdings 2	PR X
↔	Wingdings 3	PR 1
↕	Wingdings 3	PR 2
▼	Wingdings 3	PR Alt+0130
¶	Arial	PR Alt+0182
⎮	Symbols	PR Alt+0189

_____

_____

_____

for this symbol	CL this font name,	PR this or these keys
_____	_____	_____
_____	_____	_____
_____	_____	_____
_____	_____	_____
_____	_____	_____
_____	_____	_____
_____	_____	_____
_____	_____	_____
_____	_____	_____

(To create Blinky ┃ hilite the vertical line │, CL Format, CL Font, CL Engrave. In the "Color" frame CL ▼, CL Black, CL OK. CL the right margin to get │ To darken that, hilite it, CL Bold. CL the right margin to get ┃. To change the size hilite it. In the "Font Size" frame CL ▼, CL a different size, CL the right margin.)

(To create Ibby I: In the Font frame CL ▼, scroll to and CL Symbol, in the "Font Size" frame CL ▼, CL 16. Type a capital I.)

TYPE FONTS Listed and Illustrated

These are some of the available type fonts from the Character Map and Symbol panels; many of them are also on the formatting toolbar font frame list. (See "symbols, characters, and graphics" under **S.**) The names are shown in the named type font, mostly in 16 point type. Examples of special characters or capitals are shown for some type fonts. The characters can be printed as large as 72 point like the T above, and as small as 8 point like the words "Listed and Illustrated" above.

ALGERIAN ‡ § £ Œ Æ @ Þ ¡ ¢ § Û Ÿ

Arial Ä å § Ç Ô è ê Æ Ð

Arial Black £ ¥ Œ ™ Ç ç ‡ ƒ ± µ

Arial Narrow Ñ Ø ã ð ü ý

Arial Rounded MT Bold Ÿ Š ƒ £ §

Baskerville Old Face

Bauhaus 93 ABCDEFGHIJKLMNO

Bernard MT Condensed

Book Antiqua ABCDEFGHIJKLMNO

Bookman Old Style

Bradley hand itc abcdefghijkl

Braggadocio ABCDEFGHIJKLMNOPQRSTUVW

Britannic Bold ABCDEFGHIJKL

Brush Script MT   ABCDEFGH IJK

Calisto MT   ABCDEFGHIJKLMN

Century Gothic   ABCDEFGHIJKLMN

Century Schoolbook

COLONNA MT ABCDEFGHIJKLMNOPQRS

Comic Sans MS   ABCDEFGHIJKLMN

Cooper Black

Copperplate Gothic Bold

Copperplate Gothic Light

Courier New

DESDEMONA ABCDEFGHIJKLMNOPQRS

Footlight MT Light

Garamond

Haettenschweiler   **ABCDEFGHIJKLMNOPQRSTUVWXYZ**

Impact   **abcdefghijABCDEFGHIJK123**

Lucida Bright

Lucida Calligraphy   ABCDEFGH

Lucida Casual

Lucida Fax   Ä å § Ç Ô è ê Æ Ð

Lucida Handwriting   ABCDEF

matura mt script capitals abc

Mistral ABCDEFGHIJKL MN O

Modern No. 20

Monotype Corsiva ABCDEFGHIJKLMNOPQ

ONYX

P L A Y B I L L (Playbill)   A B C D E F

Trapped 1 ABCDEFGHIJKL MNOP

ψμβολ (Symbol)   ABXΔEΦΓHIϑKΛMN

Times New Roman

Tahoma   ABCDEFGHIJKLMNOPQRST

Verdana

viner hand itc   abcdefghijklm

Wide Latin   ABCDE

_____
_____
_____
_____
_____
_____
_____
_____

Appendix 5 Graphics

These are the available graphics as shown in the Character Map and the Symbol panels. (See "symbols and characters" under **S**.) They are shown here in 22 point size for clarity but they can be used either smaller or larger as desired.

Almanac MT *

Directions MT *

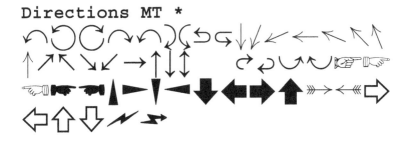

Marlett

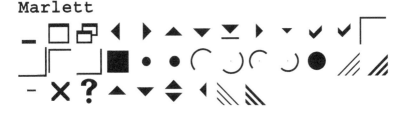

* Not included on standard Windows® Disk

MS Outlook® (Installed with Outlook®)

Webdings (Free at Microsoft® web page)

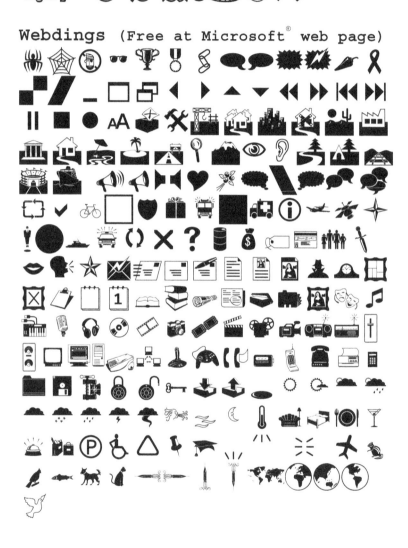

Wingdings

Wingdings 2

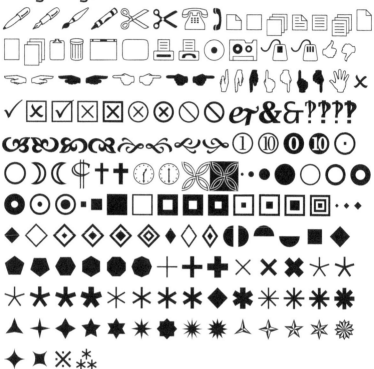

Wingdings 3

Wingdings 3 (continued)

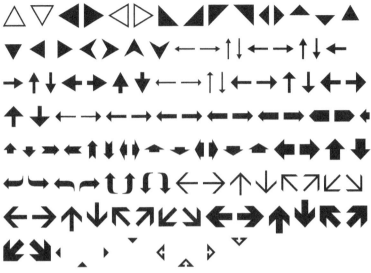

(If you don't have Webdings or one of
the Wingdings sets, they are availalable
as a free download from the Microsoft®
web page.)

_____
_____
_____
_____
_____
_____
_____
_____
_____

Appendix 6
Insert a Drawing
(or photograph) from the Clip
Art files.)

Place Blinky where you want the drawing to appear. CL Insert, CL Picture, CL "Clip Art". If a message says "Additional Clips are available on CD-ROM" CL OK. CL the "Clip Art" tab. (For photographs CL the Pictures tab.)

To find a drawing of a particular subject use the scroll bar under the "Clip Art" tab; scroll to and CL the subject you want, animals, for example. Then use the scroll bar to the right of the drawings to scroll through all the animal drawings.

To scroll through all the drawings
CL "(All Categories)" in the left scroll
bar list and use the scroll bar
to the right of the drawings. When you
find a drawing you want CL it,
CL Insert. If the drawing is available
it will appear on your document.

If you don't have a CD-ROM installed
and you CL the drawing of the elephant,
the following message will appear:
"Cannot find "F:\PUB\Clipart\
elephant.CGM". CL OK. Then the
following message will appear:
"The file 'elephant CGM' is
stored on a disk called 'Microsoft Small
Business Edition CD'. Please insert this
disk." If you have the disk insert it
and CL Retry. Otherwise
CL Cancel. On the panel titled "Cannot
Insert Picture" CL Cancel and try
another drawing.

**Change the size, shape, and location
of a drawing (or photograph)**. (When you
CL the drawing a shaded border appears
with 8 tiny boxes.)
To change size CL the drawing. Place
Ibby on the bottom right corner box
where he becomes a tilted double arrow;
CLHold and drag down and to the right
until you have the desired size.
CL the right margin.

<u>To change shape</u> CL the drawing. Place Ibby on a side or bottom box until he

becomes a horizontal or vertical double arrow. CLHold and drag to the desired shape. CL the right margin.

<u>To move the drawing</u> CL it and crossed double arrows appear. CLHold and drag to the desired position. CL the right margin.

Remove a drawing. RTCL the drawing and a menu appears. CL Cut.

See "Wrap text around a drawing." under W.

_____

_____

_____

_____

_____

_____

_____

_____

_____

_____

_____

Appendix 7   Text Boxes

A text box is a rectangle into which you can insert text, drawings, worksheets, photographs, tables, and other objects. You can change its size, shape, and location, control the inside contents, and control how text wraps around the box. You can change the border and add shading and 3D effects. You can change the direction of text inside the box and link boxes so that text flows from one box to another.

Create a text box.   CL Insert, CL "Text Box". If you are not already in the "Page Layout" view MsWord puts you there. Ibby becomes a small cross. Place the cross where you want the upper left corner of the box to be. CLHold and drag the cross down and to the right until you have traced out a box of approximately the desired size and shape. Release the mouse button.
The box appears surrounded by a shaded border and eight tiny boxes. Blinky is inside; that means the box is activated for accepting text. To deactivate the box CL outside the box. To reactivate it CL inside the box.

Remove a text box.   CL the box. Place Ibby on the border (not on a tiny box) where he becomes crossed arrows. RTCL, CL Cut.

Change the size, shape, and location of the text box.

To change the box size CL inside the box. A shaded border appears with 8 tiny boxes. Place Ibby on the bottom right corner tiny box where he becomes a tilted double arrow; CLHold and drag down and to the right (or reversed) until you have the desired size. CL outside the box.

To change the box shape CL the box. Place Ibby on one of the side or bottom tiny boxes until he becomes a horizontal or vertical double arrow. CLHold and drag to the desired shape. CL outside the box.

To move the text box place Ibby on the frame (not on a tiny box) until crossed double arrows appear. CLHold and drag to the desired position. CL outside the box.

Change the color and style of the border.
CL inside the text box. CL Format, CL "Text Box". CL the "Colors and Lines" tab. In the Line area in the Color frame CL ▼, CL the desired color. In the Style frame CL ▼, CL the desired style. For an "interrupted" border, in the Dashed frame CL ▼, CL the desired pattern.

To change the thickness of the lines,
in the Weight frame CL ▼, CL to set
the desired point size. CL OK.

Delete the border.
CL inside the text box. CL Format,
CL "Text Box". CL the "Colors and Lines"
tab. In the Line area in the Color frame
CL ▼, CL "No Line", CL OK. CL the
right margin. To avoid confusion retain
the border until all other operations
are complete.

Add a shadow, 3-D, or custom border.
With no border around the text box place
Blinky in a corner. CL Format,
CL "Borders and Shading", CL Borders.
In the Width frame CL ▼, CL the
desired line width. To try the shadow
style of border, for example, CL Shadow.
CL OK. CL the right margin.

Change direction of text inside the box.
CL inside the box, CL Format, CL "Text
Direction". In the Orientation area
CL the desired direction. CL OK. CL the
right margin.

Wrap text around the text box.
CL the box. CL Format, CL "Text Box".
On the "Format Text Box" panel CL the
Wrapping tab. CL Square, CL Right. In
the "Distance from the text" area CL 0"
top, bottom, and left and 0.1" right.
CL OK. Try other kinds of wrapping,
clearances, etc.

Use text boxes with drawings and photos.
(See "symbols, characters, & graphics"
under **S**. Also see Appendix 6 "Insert a
Drawing or Photograph from the Clip Art
Files".)
Graphics that come from the Symbols
panels and the Character Map can be
hilited and dragged in and out of the
text box.　They can be hilited and cut
or copied and then pasted in or out of
the text box. To change the size of a
symbol or character, hilite it. In the
Font Size frame CL ▼ and CL a larger or
smaller font size. CL the right margin.

From the　　**From the**　　**From**
Symbols Panel　Character Map　Clip Art

Drawings and photographs from the Clip
Art Files must be treated in a different
way. The text box must be created first;
then the Clip Art must be inserted. It
cannot be hilited or removed but it can
be controlled.　See the next paragraph.

Control Clip Art within a text box.
When you place Clip Art in a text box
there are two sets of tiny boxes
involved.　CL on the drawing and a
border with tiny black boxes appears.

CL on the inside of the box but <u>outside of the drawing</u> and the shaded border with the tiny open boxes appears. The tiny dark boxes control the drawing; the tiny open boxes control the frame. See "Change the size, shape, and location of the text box." above.

Add a background color inside the text box.
CL inside the text box. CL Format, CL "Text Box". CL the "Colors and Lines" tab. In the Fill area in the Color frame CL ▼, CL the desired color. To lighten the color so it doesn't cover up the text or graphics you want to put in the box, CL to put a check-mark in the "Transparent" checkbox. CL OK.

Link text boxes. (Let text flow from one text box to another or to several others.) Create several text boxes in a document. Place Blinky in the first box. CL View, CL Toolbars. CL "Text Box". The Text Box toolbar appears. 1.CL the text box from which you want the text to flow. 2.CL the chain on the "Text Box" toolbar (Create Text Box Link). A cup of letters appears. 3.Move the cup to the box to which you want the text to flow. If the cup spills its letters (box available) CL it. Text will now flow from the first box to the second. To add another link repeat steps 1,2,& 3.

Appendix 8   Change the Default Type Font & Margins.

If the procedures "Change the default settings for margins." or "Change the default settings for type font." under **C** fail to work then:

1.   a. With a blank page in the MsWord window CL Format, CL Font, CL the Font tab. In the Font frame scroll to and CL your desired Font. In the "Font Style" frame CL either Regular, Italic, Bold, or Bold Italic. In the Size frame CL the desired size. CL OK.

   b. CL File, CL "Page Setup", CL the "Paper Size" tab. In the "Paper Size" frame CL ▼, scroll to and CL your paper size. CL Portrait. In the "Apply to" frame CL ▼, CL "Apply to Whole Document".

   c. CL the Margins tab. Set your preferred margins. In the "Apply to" frame CL ▼, CL "Apply to Whole Document", CL OK.

2. CL File, CL "Save As". In the "File Name" frame type in a temporary name like "Oscar". In the "Save In" frame CL ▼, DBLCL (C:), DBLCL Msoffice, DBLCL Templates. With Templates in the "Save In" frame CL Save.

3. CL Start, CL Programs, CL "Windows
   Explorer". On the left side
   CL Msoffice. On the right side
   DBLCL Templates, RTCL Normal (or
   normal.dot), CL Rename. In the frame
   type "Original Normal", and DBLCL an
   open area. RTCL "Oscar", CL Rename.
   In the frame type "Normal.dot", and
   DBLCL an open area. CL **X** to close.

_____

_____

_____

_____

_____

_____

_____

_____

_____

_____

_____

_____

_____

_____

_____

_____

Appendix 9 Print Envelopes

A. Print envelopes with your choices of type font, style, size, etc.
B. If addresses are not oriented properly (when your computer doesn't recognize your printer).
C. Print an "undersized" envelope.

- -

A1. Choose the font, font size and style for your <u>return</u> address.
CL New, CL Tools, CL "Envelopes & Labels". CL the Envelopes tab. CL Options, CL the "Envelope Options" tab. In the "Return address" area CL Font.

 Scroll to and CL the Font, "Font Style", and "Font Size" that you want. CL Default, CL Yes. In the "Envelope size" frame CL ▼ , CL the desired size. (Business envelopes are Size 10 and the usual small envelope is Size 6 3/4.) CL OK.
Place Blinky in the "Return Address" frame and type your name and address. (Sometimes a long line wraps onto the next line because the "Return Address" frame is too narrow to <u>show</u> the long line properly; however, it will usually <u>print</u> it properly.) Place a test envelope in the printer and CL Print. When asked "Do you want to save the new return address as the default return address?" CL Yes.

If the return address is printed too close to the top of the envelope add a blank line (or two) to your return address in the "Return Address" frame.

A2.   Print the envelopes.

1. Make a list of the required addresses in the following format and in the font, font type and size you want on the envelopes: (For long lists put them into several columns on the page.)

Mr. John Jones
1234 Shady Drive
Missoula, Montana 45678

Mr. Frank Smith
5678 34th Street
New York, NY 12345   *etc.*

```
┌─────────────────────────────┐
│ xxxxx                   ┌──┐ │
│ xxxxx                   │  │ │
│ xxxxx                   └──┘ │
│      xx xxx xxxxxx           │
│      xxxxxxxxxxx             │
│      xxxxxxxx.xx xxxxx       │
└─────────────────────────────┘
```

Save the list as "Envelope Address List".

2. Open "Envelope Address List". CL Edit, CL "Select All". CL Cut, CL New, CL Paste.

3. Scroll to and hilite the first address to be printed. (If you are using an address list that includes phone numbers and e-mail addresses be careful not to hilite more than the desired address.)

3   Appendix 9   Print Envelopes

CL Tools, CL "Envelopes and Labels". The desired address and return address will appear. (Sometimes a long line wraps onto the next line because the "Delivery Address" frame is too narrow to show the long line properly; however, it will often print it properly. If the Omit checkbox has a checkmark CL to delete it.

4. Insert an envelope into the printer. CL Print.

5. Repeat paragraphs 3 and 4 as required.

A3.   Print a single line of large type instead of a delivery address: If you try to copy a single line from the address list the program won't accept it. Create the desired line and then type "mm" on the next line. Hilite the two lines, proceed as in **A2** above. When the two lines appear in the "Delivery Address" frame erase the "mm" and proceed. If you do not want to print the return address CL to put a check in the Omit checkbox.

B. What to do when the addresses are not properly oriented on the envelope.
CL Tools, Cl "Envelopes and Labels",
CL the Envelopes tab. CL Options,
CL the "Printing Options" tab. You must
CL one of the six drawings, choose Face
Up or Face Down, choose Clockwise
Rotation or not.
(If your printer feeds from the top
pretend the drawings are upside down.)

The questions are now:
1. Does your printer want the envelopes
   fed face up or face down?
2. Does your printer want the envelopes
   fed length-wise or crosswize?
3. Does your printer want the envelopes
   fed in the middle of the paper slot
   or at an edge.

The answer to question 1 tells you
whether to CL for Face Up or Face Down.
The answer to question 2 eliminates
three of the six drawings.
The answer to question 3 leaves only one
or two of the drawings possible.

If you try the remaining possible
drawings with the Clockwise Rotation and
then without the Clockwise Rotation you
should find the proper setting for you.
Unfortunately you will have to redo the
settings each time you print an
envelope, so **be sure to record them for
future use.**

5 Appendix 9 Print Envelopes

C. Print an "undersized" envelope.

If you are a do-it-yourself greeting card maker you fold a standard piece of 8 1/2 x 11 inch paper twice to create a format for a greeting card that measures 4 1/4 x 5 1/2.

Size 5 1/2 envelopes that are used for announcements and invitations are perfect for just such a card. However, Windows thinks they are too small to print and many printers will not accept them.

The easiest way around that is to print the return address and addressees address on separate 1 x 2 5/8 inch labels and attach the labels to the small envelopes by hand.

(See Appendix 2, "Print Labels".)

If you <u>must</u> print the small envelopes try this:

1. When setting the envelope size CL C6.

2. When typing the return address in the "Return Address" frame <u>leave eight blank spaces at the left of each line</u>. That moves the return address to the right to compensate for the smaller envelope and fools the printer into thinking it is printing the longer envelope. (<u>Don't put any spaces in front of any wrapped partial lines.</u>)

Appendix 10 Tables
Create forms, fill them in, and have them calculate for you.

Create a simple blank table form.

In this table form each small rectangle is a cell. A group of cells from left to right is a row. A group of cells from top to bottom is a column.
To create such a table form: CL Table, CL "Insert Table". CL to set the number of columns (4 shown), CL to set the number of rows (3 shown), CL to set the column width (1 inch shown). CL OK. (Let the automatic feature set the height of the rows; if the type is too large or the entry is too long the cell will increase in height.)

Change the width of all the columns.
Place Blinky somewhere in the table. CL Table, CL "Cell Height and Width". CL the Column tab, set the desired width.

Add, delete or move a row.
Add a row. Place Blinky in the bottom right cell and PR the Tab key.
Delete a row. Place Blinky in the row, CL Table, CL "Select Row", CL Cut.

<u>Move a row.</u> Place the arrow to the left
of the row you want to move and CL.
(The row becomes hilited.) Place the
arrow in the leftmost cell of the
hilited row and CLHold and Drag the
arrow to the leftmost cell of the row
you want to be above. Release. CL the
right margin.
Caution: In some versions of MsWORD an
entire row will vanish when you attempt
to move the row as explained above.
PR Ctrl+Z to restore the missing row.
Then CL outside the table to the left of
the row you want to move. (That row
becomes hilited.) CLHold inside the row
and drag the arrow to place it at the
left-most edge in the left-most cell
of the row on top of which you want
to place the moved row. Release the
mouse button.
In some programs you can move the row up
but not down. If that is the case move
other rows up to create the down move
for the desired row.

Add, delete or move a column.
<u>Add a column to the right of the table</u>:
Place Ibby outside of and to the right
of the top right cell. CLHold and drag
down to create a hilite to the right
of the table. (When you do that the
"Insert Table" button on the standard

toolbar changes to the "Insert Columns"
button.) CL the "Insert Columns" button,
CL the right margin.

Add a column anywhere else. Place Ibby
in the top cell of the column to the
right of where you want to add a column.
CLHold and drag down to hilite all the
cells in the column. (When you do that
the "Insert Table" button on the
standard toolbar changes to the "Insert
Columns" button.) CL the "Insert
Columns" button, CL the right margin.

Delete a column. Place Ibby in the
top cell of the column. CLHold and
drag down to hilite all the cells
in the column.CL Cut.

Move a column. Place Ibby in the top
cell of the column. CLHold and drag down
to hilite all the cells in the column.
Place the arrow inside the column.
CLHold and drag the column
to the new location.

_____

_____

_____

_____

_____

_____

_____

_____

Change the height of a row.
When you place Ibby on a horizontal line
in the table he turns into two short
horizontal lines and two short vertical
arrows; call that pattern the **horizontal
clamp**. To change the height of a row
place the horizontal clamp on a
horizontal line, CLHold and drag the
line up or down.

Change the width of a column.
When you place Ibby on a vertical line
in the table he turns into two short
vertical lines and two short horizontal
arrows; let us call that pattern the
vertical clamp. There are three methods
for changing the width of a column:

**1. Change the width of only the chosen
column, displacing everything to the
right of the chosen column and thereby
changing the overall width of the table.**
First PRHold the Shift key. Place the
vertical clamp on the vertical line that
forms the right edge of that column,
CLHold, drag the line to the right or
left and release.

**2. Change the width of the chosen column
and change the width of the column to the
right in the opposite sense, retaining
the overall width of the table.**

Place the **vertical clamp** on the vertical
line that forms the right edge of that
column, CLHold, drag the line to the
right or left and release.

**3. Change the width of the chosen column
and change the widths of <u>all</u> the columns
to the right in the opposite sense,
retaining the overall width of the
table.**
<u>First PRHold the Ctrl key.</u> Place the
vertical clamp on the vertical line that
forms the right edge of that column,
CLHold, drag the line to the right, and
release.
(If you change the width of the last
column on the right the overall width of
the table changes.)

**Align the table left, centered, or
right.**   Place the arrow outside of and
to the left of the top cell. CLHold and
drag straight down until the entire
table is hilited.
<u>Do not hilite beyond the table.</u> On the
formatting toolbar CL one of the three
alignment buttons to move the table to
the left margin, to center it, or to
move it to the right margin. CL the
right margin.
Note that <u>to insert text to the left
or right of the table</u> you must use a
text box as described in Appendix 7.

Move the table up, down, or to a new page.
Place Ibby in the upper left cell. CLHold and drag down and to the right to hilite the entire table. CL Cut. Place Ibby where you want the table to be. CL Paste.

Modify the blank table form. Place Blinky inside the table. CL the "Tables and Borders" button on the Standard tool-bar; the "Tables and Borders" toolbar appears with 1) a pencil for drawing more lines, 2) an eraser for erasing lines, 3) a choice of simple lines, double lines, wavy lines, etc., 4) a choice of line widths and colors, 5) ability to change the direction of the text, and more.

Add extra lines: When you CL the "Tables and Borders" button the cursor becomes a pencil. If you lose the pencil CL the "Draw Table" button (pencil button) on the "Tables and Borders" toolbar. Place the pencil point inside the table where you want to start a line, CLHold, drag to an intersection and release.

Change the line width: In the "Line Weight" frame CL ▼ , CL a different weight and use the pencil as described above.

<u>Change from a single line to a double line or something more fancy</u>: In the "Line Style" frame CL ▼ , scroll to and CL a different line style. Place the pencil where you want to start the change, CLHold and drag to an intersection. Release.

<u>To erase a line</u>: CL the Eraser button, place the eraser where you want to start to erase, CLHold and drag to a line intersection, and release. CL the right margin to remove the eraser. Explore these and other options on the "Tables and Borders" toolbar to create more distinctive tables.

Create "designer" tables.
You can easily create tables that are contemporary, or elegant, or profes-sional, etc. CL Table, CL "Insert Table", CL Auto-Format. In the Formats frame scroll to and CL a format; a sample of the style appears in the preview frame. Put checkmarks in the checkboxes to use any or all of the available features. CL OK. CL to set the number of columns and the number of rows and CL to set the column width. CL OK.

Entrant	Saturday Scores	Sunday Scores	Combined Scores
Jones	342	256	598
Smith	305	296	601

Fill in the blank form.
Place Blinky in a cell and type an entry.
To move from one cell to another use the Tab key or the Arrow keys. The text in each cell can be aligned to the left, centered, aligned right, or justified. (Note that in the table above the titles and the scores are centered while the list of entrants are aligned to the left.

Change the alignment of the text in a cell. Place the arrow in the cell, CL to hilite the cell and CL one of the Alignment buttons on the formatting toolbar.

Change the alignment of the text in a group of cells. Place Ibby in the topmost cell you want to change, CLHold and drag down to hilite all the cells you want to change, CL the desired alignment button.

Appendix 10 Tables 9

Perform calculations in the table.
One can take numbers from certain cells,
perform calculations on them, and
present the result in another cell. To
do that every cell in the table must be
identified by the column and row in
which it lies. The columns are letters
and the rows are numbers. Each cell is
identified as shown.

Column	A	B	C	D
Row 1	A1	B1	C1	D1
Row 2	A2	B2	C2	D2
Row 3	A3	B3	C3	D3

Note that to put text next to a table
you have to enclose it in a text box as
explained in Appendix 7.

Assume that you have the following
table:

	A	B	C	D	E	F	G
1		Mon	Tue	Wed	Thu	Fri	Tot
2	Jones	12	14	11	15	16	
3	Smith	14	11	16	14	11	

To fill in the total for Jones direct
the program to calculate the sum of all
the numbers in cells B2 through F2:
Place Blinky in cell G2. CL Table,
CL Formula. In the Formula frame type
=SUM(B2:F2) , CL OK and the total, 68,
will appear.

10   Appendix 10   Tables

For Smith's total place Blinky in cell
G3. CL Table, CL Formula. In the Formula
frame type =SUM(B3:F3) , CL OK and 66
appears.

Codes for cells and combinations of cells.

Now that you see how easy it is here are
the codes that will help you master the
art of tabular calculations.

For example:

B4	means the cell in column B row 4.
2:2	means all the cells in row 2. If cell A2 is a title cell be sure it contains no numbers.
C2:F2	means the cells in row 2 starting at column C and ending at column F.
B:B	means all the cells in column B. If B1 is a title cell be sure it contains no numbers.
B2:B6	means the cells in column B starting at row 2 and ending at row 6.

Formulas for calculations where cells or numbers or x% must be in the parentheses.

Addition	=SUM( )
Show the maximum	=MAX( )
Show the minimum	=MIN( )
Calculate the Average	=AVERAGE( )
Multiply the cells	=PRODUCT( )

Appendix 10 Tables

To illustrate the use of the formulas
and the cells here is a table and all
the formulas used to create it.

1A DAYS	B JONES SCORES	C SMITH SCORES	D JONES & SMITH SCORES
2 Mon	40	45	
3 Tues	25	30	
4 Wed	15	11	
5 Thurs	33	28	
6 Fri	12	14	
7 Total	125	128	253
8 Maximum	40	45	45
9 Minimum	12	11	11
10 Average	25	25.6	25.3
11 Max X 5	200	225	

CELL	FORMULA	CELL	FORMULA
B7	=SUM(B2:B6)	C7	=SUM(C2:C6)
B8	=MAX(B2:B6)	C8	=MAX(C2:C6)
B9	=MIN(B2:B6)	C9	=MIN(C2:C6)
B10	=AVE(B2:B6	C10	=AVE(C2:C6)
B11	=PROD([B8],5)	C11	=PROD([C8],5)
D7	=SUM(B7:C7)	D9	=MIN(B9:C9)
D8	=MAX(B8:C8)	D10	=AVE(B10:C10)

About The Author

Bob Ginsberg was born in Grand Forks, North Dakota in 1925. At Central High School he edited his 1942 class year-book, appeared on a weekly student radio program, worked on the school newspaper, directed a play with an all girl cast, won a number of speech and essay contests, and wrote, produced, directed, and starred in a variety show.

During World War II he graduated from high school at age 17 and enlisted in the Army Air Corps, earning a commission as a 2nd Lt. and Navigator's wings. At 19 he was with the 15th Air Force in southern Italy where he flew 13 missions in a B-24 Liberator bomber.

After World War II he attended the University of Minnesota and in 1949 was awarded the B.A., Magna cum Laude, Phi Beta Kappa, in Physics, Philosopy, and Math. He then went to the Institute of Optics at the University of Rochester, New York, where in 1951 he received an M.S. in Optics and Applied Optics.

He designed microscopes and telescopes for Bausch & Lomb Optical Co.. He was a Senior Scientist at Hughes Aircraft Co. for nineteen years, helped produce the cameras that the Surveyor spacecrafts landed on the moon in 1966, and worked on a variety of space and military programs there.

Since 1982 he has been a consultant in Optical and Optomechanical Engineering under the name Optics Expertise. He has consulted for Hughes Aircraft Co. and a number of other technical firms designing space, scientific, and commercial optics (but no eyeglasses).

At the age of 75 he still plays piano by ear (George Gershwin, Jerome Kern, Hoagy Carmichael, etc.) and plays a credible game of tennis doubles.

His antipathy for computing began in 1950 when everyone designed lenses using mechanical calculators and thick books of trigonometric tables.

He decided to buy a computer so he could e-mail his nieces and nephews. For two weeks before the arrival of his computer he had tried to learn about computers by reading the 400 page books and the 200 page reference books; he was disappointed with their lack of clarity.

After receiving the computer, once he figured out how something worked he jotted down the steps on a note pad in words he could readily understand. He then decided to incorporate all the note pads into a reference manual for his own use. Eight weeks after his first contact with a computer book and six weeks after his first contact with a computer the first draft of his reference manual was completed.

.

www.ingramcontent.com/pod-product-compliance
Lightning Source LLC
Chambersburg PA
CBHW051053050326
40690CB00006B/701